# KALEIDOSCOPE OF COLORS

*Advancing the Kingdom
by Reflecting God's Light*

By Christi Johnston

# Endorsements

Psalm 37:25 eludes to the fact that age is followed after youth and God's faithfulness is proven in both the young and the old sections of life. I too was once young and in that youth I observed the faithfulness of my children and the children of the churches I pastored. As I grew older they advanced in years as well. I was moving off the scene and they were moving onto the scene.

The book you hold in your hand came into existence due to the prophetic ministry of one of my daughters (Marla Austin Nelson) to one of my church kids (Christi Pack Johnston). Both of these ladies have moved from Children's Church to big church and are finding their place in a powerful flow of the Holy Spirit's anointing. Christi has stood in, and is still going through, the fire as proof that God's grace is sufficient for every event of life. She is an inspiration to so many who know her and to whom she ministers.

This book has not fallen into your hands by accident. It is no doubt a link in this ministry chain that started in these ladies and will be passed along to you as you read. The anointing passes from generation to generation and this work and its author proves that that same anointing can flow to you as well. In HIS service,

— **Evangelist/Pastor Sam Austin**

Christi Johnston is a relentless pursuer of truth and a proclaimer of God's promises. I found myself nodding my head throughout the book as I read. Her words resonate with those of us who believe yet trust in God's ability to make beauty from ashes.

She is a bright light for God's Kingdom here on earth! Christi shares some incredible stories of herself and others, using their lives to bring light and hope to a lost world. She also offers solid biblical teaching and encouragement to spend time with Jesus and know the Word in order to effectively reflect God's light.

Ultimately you will be inspired to be used by the Lord, no matter where you are in life. "You can reflect His light in all you do."

— **Rachel Scott**
*Singer songwriter/worship leader /writer*


While Noah built the ark, he must have felt foolish, even discouraged at times. Think of it: he was told what to do by God, but his friends, neighbors, even family must have thought it quite comical. "Hey, there goes crazy Noah, hauling more lumber."

Yet Noah persisted because he saw what no one else saw—the vision of the Lord—and he built accordingly. Those around Noah only saw the lumber and the labor. So they did what ignorant people do: they mocked, they reviled, and ultimately they ignored. (Ignored…ignorant.)

We Christians are called to a mysterious union with God our Father through His Son, Jesus Christ. We know it involves salvation and God's Spirit, but how well do we see God's vision for our lives? How well do we know God's endgame?

On the surface, we are living the prescribed Christian life. We pray the prayers, sing the songs, and attend the meetings. We haul lumber, stack it in place, and live our lives as best we can. But do we know what we are building? What is God really building?

In *Kaleidoscope of Colors: Advancing the Kingdom by Reflecting God's Light*, Christi Johnston shares her vision for God's endgame. We are not here to endure, to conform, to wait for heaven. We are called for more. We are receptors of light, shining forth into the darkness, even when the darkness cannot comprehend it.

We are colors. We are rainbows. We are the lark ascending, rising on the wings of song. We are beautiful. We are God's creation.

As Noah built the ark, he saw what no one else saw. Not the boat; not the rain; not the flood…but the rainbow. Noah saw the reason for the ark. God's endgame was a new earth, and this gave glory to Noah's efforts.

God sees your destiny. Let Him prepare you. He, and He alone, knows what's ahead. The principles in Christi's book are part of that preparation. Embrace them! And receive God's glory.

"Dear friends, now we are children of God, and what we will be has not yet been made known. But we know that when Christ appears, we shall be like him, for we shall see him as he is" (1 John 3:2, NIV).

— **Clay Nash, Apostle**
*Leader, Author, Teacher*

Today I tried to remember my first encounter with Christi Johnston, and I don't think this was the first, but it was memorable. Let's go there.

Nashville, Tennessee, the year was probably 2007 or 2008. My daughter Kelly had befriended Christi and constantly told me about this amazing girl from Arkansas. She had invited her friend to come hang out and fellowship. Kelly and Christi had been road buddies for a while. When you travel and do ministry like we have always done, we had our people. Those special people who felt like family, the ones that your brain and soul agreed on. She was one of those, and we welcomed her into the SMALL club of the trusted.

As we sat at a downtown Nashville restaurant, loving our salads and bread, Christi began to pour out. She began to tell me her story. I listened. I realized that her gifts would take her far and that her compassion would allow her to walk into additional rooms. She wasn't average. She sparkled. She was beautiful, smart, and walked in so much humility it was tangible. All in all, she was different.

I meet thousands of people and love them all. However, when I meet someone like Christi, I realize that the blessing was mine. Her walk with Jesus will be a forever gift to me. She understands the battle and is willing to go to war with me, for me, and takes her weapons when she goes!

She's suffered great things, yet her smile lights up a room. Her life is far from glamorous, yet she carries THAT shine and encourages everyone she encounters. The level of anxiety that she is faced with would cripple most, yet she pours herself into studying and writing. She reflects His light, and yes, I love the name of this book. It's perfect!

*Kaleidoscope of Colors* will speak to you. Let it challenge you, change you, and allow you to see life from Christi's world. She understood the assignment. If you only read one book this year, this is it!

— **Kathy Crabb Hannah**


Many of us talk a good talk but few walk the real walk of a surrendered life in Christ. One of those few is my friend Christi Johnston. I have witnessed Christi give of herself over and over again until all that's left is her hand in Jesus' hand helping her get through the next hour. It is in this place of complete exhaustion that Christi has come through shining with the Lord's glory, evident for anyone to see.

I believe you will find some rich treasures in her latest book, *Kaleidoscope of Colors*. I know I did. An abundance of real treasures that you can use to deepen your walk with the Lord are found in just the first chapter. I know that most of us in this crazy, hectic world have very little extra time to read, but I promise you, this is one book that is certainly well worth your time. I know you will enjoy *Kaleidoscope of Colors* as much as I have. Blessings as you begin the journey.

— **Representative Mary Bentley**
*Member of the Arkansas House of Representatives*

I hope you will not only read this book, but you will study this book. Christi Johnston does a wonderful job encouraging believers to rise up and reflect God's light. The key is being available for Kingdom business. If you are too busy for God, you have your priorities out of order. Compelled by her passion to see souls born again, she shares her heart as she encourages others to shine His light brighter than ever before. This book will challenge you to have bold faith, let your light shine brightly, and push you towards your own spiritual destiny.

— **The Honorable Jason Rapert**
*Founder & President of the*
*National Association of Christian Lawmakers*

© 2024 Christi Johnston

*Kaleidoscope of Colors*
by Christi Johnston

Printed in the United States of America

ISBN: 9798324739027

All rights reserved. No part of this document may be reproduced or transmitted in any form, by any means (electronic, photocopying, recording, or otherwise) without the written permission of the author.

Published by: Michael Young Publishing

$\left[ \text{M}\mathbf{Y}\text{P} \right]$

The King James Version (KJV). Public domain.

The New King James Version® (NKJV). Copyright © 1982 by Thomas Nelson. Used by permission. All rights reserved.

The Holy Bible, New Living Translation (NLT). Copyright © 1996, 2004, 2015 by Tyndale House Foundation. Used by permission of Tyndale House Publishers, Inc., Carol Stream, Illinois 60188. All rights reserved.

The Holy Bible, English Standard Version. ESV®. Text Edition: 2016. Copyright © 2001 by Crossway Bibles, a publishing ministry of Good News Publishers.

The Holy Bible, New International Version®, NIV®. Copyright ©1973, 1978, 1984, 2011 by Biblica, Inc.® Used by permission. All rights reserved worldwide.

The Christian Standard Bible (CSB). Copyright © 2017 by Holman Bible Publishers. Used by permission. Christian Standard Bible®, and CSB® are federally registered trademarks of Holman Bible Publishers, all rights reserved.

# Dedication

I dedicate this book to my Lord and Savior, Jesus Christ. My earnest prayer is that you will be readily available for Kingdom use. If you are willing, He will turn you as a Kaleidoscope to reflect His glory. Your life is a living epistle, live it well.

# Table of Contents

Foreword .................................................................................. xii

Introduction ............................................................................ xiv

Chapter 1: Color Me Happy .................................................... 1

Chapter 2: A Gentle Turn ...................................................... 18

Chapter 3: Mirrors ................................................................. 35

Chapter 4: I'll Say Yes, Lord, Yes ........................................... 47

Chapter 5: Rest Is a Weapon ................................................. 62

Chapter 6: Shine Bright ......................................................... 74

Chapter 7: Beautiful Patterns ................................................ 88

Chapter 8: Faces .................................................................... 99

Chapter 9: Moments, Memories, and Mandates ................ 110

Chapter 10: Kingdom Assignments ..................................... 121

Afterword ............................................................................. 129

About the Author ................................................................ 130

# Foreword

Rock candy and a kaleidoscope.

That was my purchase in a sundries store at a New Jersey Turnpike rest stop (probably a diversion tactic by my parents to keep their eight-year-old occupied for the remainder of our road trip). I walked outside to the parking lot, popped the candy in my mouth, and held the kaleidoscope to my eye and toward the sun. I twisted it this way and that…this way and that…this way and that. Although over fifty years ago, I still remember the dazzling delight that toy kaleidoscope brought me.

A kaleidoscope is a cylinder that produces patterns of color using pieces of glass reflected in mirrors. What would it look like to live a kaleidoscope life and emit an array of color in a world where most view life as gray?

Jesus.

It would also resemble the life of one of His followers, Christi Johnston. Christi is a beautiful, godly woman. But her spirit exudes her outward beauty, a result of time spent cultivating a deep, intimate relationship with Jesus. He has given her joy instead of mourning, beauty in place of ashes, and purpose in the pain.

How we handle suffering, success, and setbacks determines whether we emanate Jesus' life, beauty, and magnificence. He wants to utilize all we've been through to transform us into His image. Christi has let Him. She views every situation in life through the lens of Scripture, holds up every experience to the light of the Holy Spirit, and consequently mirrors her Savior.

*Kaleidoscope of Colors* will deepen your walk with Jesus. (Spoiler alert: it's wonderful!) My advice to you is to read it slowly, reflectively, and prayerfully. Give the Holy Spirit time and space to fashion you into a vessel bearing the image of Jesus. Let Christi's God encounters and prophetic revelations become yours.

Let Christi Johnston help you join your story (small s) with His story (capital S), so that your story (small s) will have a redemptive final chapter and be filled with a…*Kaleidoscope of Colors*.

**—Dr. Jamie Morgan**
*Director of Trailblazer Mentoring Network*
*Mentor to Women in Ministry*
*TrailblazerMentoring.com*

# Introduction

In my daily prayer time, I always ask the Lord to turn me each day for Kingdom use. I pray: Search me and know me, create in me a clean heart and a right spirit. If there be any sin in my heart, forgive me and let me be used as a vessel of honor for Your glory.

The Word says: whatsoever you ask in faith believing, He will answer. I am proof that He will do what He says He will do. He allows people to cross my path that are in need of Him. It is a divine appointment as He sends those to me that desperately need an encounter with Him.

I wrote this book to encourage others to allow Jesus to use you where you are at. Your life is a living, breathing testimony. The only Bible some may ever read is by watching you walk out your faith. The consistency in your love walk allows others to see that no matter what, you will not to quit. In Proverbs 24:10 it states: "If you faint in the day of adversity, your strength is small" (KJV). I do not want small faith or small strength!

Our goal in our Christian walk should be to "add on" daily. We are to be lifetime learners ever growing in the knowledge of His truth. When we stop growing, we stop sharing. The Great Commission commands us to: "Go ye into all the world and preach the

Gospel." Now is not the time to water down our faith or to have small faith. It is high time the church rises up and becomes the bride He has called us to be.

Jesus Christ is not coming back for a weak, anemic, sick bride. He is coming back to a glorious bride that is without spot, blemish, or wrinkle. A bride that is alive and well, carrying the Gospel to a lost and dying world.

I want to be a part of this end-time harvest and I want each of you to be as well. In Matthew 9:37 Jesus said to His disciples, "The harvest is plentiful but the laborers are few" (ESV).

Are you willing to labor with me? If so, ask the Lord to equip you with great strength as you say YES to His call. Every single day, ask Him to place someone in your path that you can encourage with the Gospel. Wherever you may be at, whether it is work, a ballgame, the grocery store, etc., I can guarantee you there is someone waiting on you to do what He has called you to do.

Step out in boldness and allow Him to use you for Kingdom business.

# Chapter 1

## COLOR ME HAPPY

On February 17, 2012, on the floor of a little hometown beauty salon, my life shifted. A precious lady named Marla Austin prophesied over me. As she ministered, it was as if a river of living water poured out of her soul into mine. She told me she saw me as a "kaleidoscope of colors."

In detail, she described how I would be used daily to serve the Kingdom. With each gentle turn, a reflection of His light would shine. She spoke these words over me, "One day you might want to be on the mission field preaching in Africa. The next day you might want to rock babies, or better yet, while styling someone's hair, you will begin to pray over them as the Spirit moves. You will minister all over the world, giving glory to God.

"I say to you these words: 'Be ready, if you are available for His use and you are, big things will happen. Souls will be added to the Kingdom daily. Your obedience will turn into a lifetime of victories.'"

I had written the prophecy down word for word in an old, brown leather journal. I would pull it out and read it over and over. I prayed over it and asked Jesus to let it be so. That was over twelve years ago and every single word that she prophesied over me is coming to pass even as I type this. A prophetic word given, a prophetic word received. I am willing, I am available, I am a kaleidoscope.

I have always been fascinated with color. I distinctly remember when I was in elementary school and learned my primary colors. I practiced going over ROYGBIV[1] in my head for hours upon hours. Surely everyone else learned it that way too. Back then, I thought that was the coolest thing ever. We even sang the colors in song form, and to this day, I can still sing it.

One of my classmates had the neatest Crayola colors I had ever seen. It was a small square box with 120 crayons inside. It folded up into a small container that could fit into a backpack pocket. I, on the other hand, had a huge box of colors that sat directly on top of my desk. I remember thinking, *Wow, his family must be rich.*

I laugh as I type this because I never forgot it. I was jealous because his colors were much better than mine. The case was cool, the colors were brighter, and he could fold it into a compact and tuck it away. Mine were cheap, broken, and dull. Isn't that like life?

---

1   Wikipedia, ROYGBIV is an acronym for the sequence of hues in a rainbow: red, orange, yellow, green, blue, indigo, and violet, https://en.wikipedia.org/wiki/ROYGBIV.

Maybe life is dull in color to you right now. In my experience, when you go through a hard season, color disappears. Everything just goes gray. You don't see the brightness of color because visual details are muted by circumstances of life.

Do you look at your neighbor and compare your colors to theirs? It happens. We all do it from time to time. I need to remind you though, that we are all a little broken, but the last time I checked, broken crayons still color the same.

The world at this very moment seems to be living in muted colors. End-time prophecy is being fulfilled before our eyes, therefore people are on heightened alert. Emotions are on the rise, offense is at hand, and disrespect like never before. The fulfillment of the Word is coming to pass ever so quickly. Instead of focusing on God's promises, people focus on the problems. They are broken, confused, anxious, and afraid.

Hosea 4:6 states, "My people are destroyed for lack of knowledge." In order to take God at His Word, you have to know the Word. We must diligently seek Him and apply wisdom to our lives. God is a Promise Keeper. If He said it, I believe it.

I have found that people often expect too much from people and too little from God. Only God can be God and people can only be people. I have stood on God's promises for well over twenty years and counting. I don't always understand the way He chooses to do things, but I have learned I don't have to. I have trained myself to allow my faith to speak so loudly that I can't even hear what fear is saying.

Isaiah 5:20 states, "Woe unto them that call evil good, and good evil; that put darkness for light, and light for darkness; that put bitter for sweet, and sweet for bitter" (KJV). The master deceiver himself, satan, loves to take the truth of God's Word and counterfeit it. Since he was kicked out of heaven, he roams to and fro, attempting to devour the saints. I say "attempt" for he only has as much power as we allow him to have. The Word says that we as believers have been given ALL power and authority over him.

Proverbs 16:18: "Pride goes before destruction, and a haughty spirit before a fall" (NKJV). This is exactly what happened to satan. He rebelled against God and thought he should have the same respect as God or even try to be God. His prideful and haughty spirit took him completely out of heaven. Same goes for us today. When we flaunt pride and arrogance, we go down quickly. John 12:43 tells us, "For they loved human praise more than the praise of God" (NLT).

There are so many promises in the Word, but I want to focus on one in particular. Let's look at the story of Noah. In Genesis chapter 6, God looked down on the human race and saw (just like today) wickedness, violence, and evil everywhere. He decided to destroy all living things on the earth, except for Noah, who had found grace in the eyes of the Lord.

God instructed Noah to build an ark with certain precision and to take two of every sort of animal into the ark. When Noah was 600 years old, God released the rains that lasted forty days and forty nights, which caused the flood. Noah and his wife, sons, and their wives, along with the animals he took aboard the ark, were spared the flood and survived. But every living thing outside of the ark was destroyed in the waters of the flood.

When the ark eventually came to rest, he sent a raven out of the ark to search for dry land, and then a dove. The dove returned, and then he sent it out again. This happened several times before the dove eventually returned with an olive branch in its mouth, a symbol of peace ever since.

In Genesis 9:13, God showed Noah the rainbow He had set in the clouds. He told Noah this was His covenant with man, that He would never flood the earth again. A beautiful promise was given to us, and the enemy of our souls has tried to contaminate the promise.

As you look around in the world today and see the beautiful colors of the rainbow, the believer sees the promise. Sadly, the nonbelievers see it as the most powerful symbol of PRIDE. They have taken the Word of God and twisted it to their very own destruction.

For every real promise there is a real counterfeit that tries to exalt itself above the Lord our God. This particular group would say the rainbow reflects the diversity of the Pride community and the "spectrum" of human sexuality and gender. The Pride flag proclaims to them: "This is who I am."

I don't believe God was confused when He created man. He created Adam as a living being, in His image, and gave him authority over everything else He created. Man was created to be the physical carrier of God's Spirit in the earth.

Part of human nature is that we, as living beings like Adam, have a free will. God is too loving to force submission from anyone. He wants us to freely choose to love and serve Him. The problem with this ideology is the "free will" part.

Our flesh is enmity against our spirit, and if it doesn't satisfy our flesh, our "free will" wants to rebel. My husband was raised "Free Will Baptist." He tells the story of how he did everything his "Free Will" wanted to do. I don't think he got it. (Pun intended.)

This is why it is so very important to know who God says that we are. We are not who this world says we are or what are flesh tells us to "identify" as. Our identity is found in Christ Jesus alone.

Confusion is a tool of the enemy. He uses that tool to twist and turn our minds. Satan does not want us to be happy, free, or blessed. He clearly wants us to be sad, bound, and defeated. First Corinthians 14:33 tells us that God is not the author of confusion but of peace. So anything that brings confusion to our life is not from God but the enemy. As a born-again believer, you have the mind of Christ.

Remember, the Lord has not given you the spirit of fear but of power, of love, and a sound mind. If our mind is not sound, then we can't carry His glory to a lost and dying world. As we read, pray, worship, and study, we fill our vessels to be able to pour out to others. We cannot pour from an empty cup, therefore we fill ourselves first, then we can pour His spirit out to others.

The goal is to be so full of the love of Christ that others receive joy when they are around us. This opens the door for you to witness to them. We should be so joyful and loving that others might say, "I don't know what it is that they have, but I want it."

I believe the greatest gospel we could ever preach is the way we live our life. Are we faithful in the good and the bad times? When we are in the valley, do we still praise or do we complain? Noah didn't stop to explain himself to the unbelievers. He let the rain do the talking. He trusted what the Lord had told him. He built the ark exactly as he was instructed, and in the end it brought safety to his family.

Life is full of struggles and disappointments, but what we focus on we magnify. I refuse to focus on all the bad things in this world for it steals my joy where I can't see the good. The catch phrase "color me happy" stems from when you are sad, color disappears. You don't see it because visual details are muted by sorrow.

It is said that the brighter and lighter a color, the more happy and optimistic it will make you feel. I believe that to be true. When I wear brighter colors, I feel more joyful. It's crazy how color can literally change your mood. Today is a bright, sunny day and my mood is always lifted when it is.

One of my favorite Scriptures is found in Psalm 3:3, "But You, O Lord, are a shield around me, my glory, and the lifter of my head." On days that I don't feel happy, Jesus lifts my head high. I can look all around me and see His beautiful creation that is full of splendor.

One thing I want to encourage each of you in is to allow joy and sorrow to coexist. This is something I have had to learn to do having a medically complex child. The enemy would love for me to live a defeated life, but I choose to stand on the promises of God's Word.

Some days are full of sunshine while other days are gray. We must embrace every day with gladness no matter what it looks like. It can be gray and gloomy outside, but the joy of the Lord can shine bright amidst the clouds.

This week my daughter Hannah had so many seizures. It is extremely hard to watch your child suffer and you can't do anything to fix it. She is my greatest blessing and her life reflects the light of Jesus beautifully. It is our duty as born-again believers to reflect the light of Christ in our lives. When we are available for Kingdom use, He turns us each day to reflect Him.

I believe the greatest message we can ever preach is to fully live our lives surrendered to Christ. Daily, we should wake up and ask the Lord these questions:

- What can I do to be a difference maker for the Kingdom?

- Who can I serve and be a blessing to?

- Will You place a hungry soul on my heart or in my path to minister Your love?

I am willing and available for Kingdom use today, Jesus. Turn me to reflect Your light today and every day. May the words of my mouth and the meditations of my heart be pure, holy, and true as I extend Your love and grace to others.

I recall a story of a young lady that I would like to share about. I won't use her real name but let's call her Katy. Katy loved the Lord with all her heart, mind, soul, and strength. She was raised in church with great faith and lived it out loud until she met Susan. Susan was a sweet girl who had a profession of faith but no personal relationship with Jesus. I was just the observer in this, but we all know the fruit does the talking, right?

Katy was happy, blessed, and bore much fruit until Susan became her friend. I watched a slow fade in Katy. It wasn't overnight, nor did I witness her turn off her light; it just grew dim. My heart hurt as I watched this bright, shining star that shined the light of Jesus, literally walk into darkness. This once joyful, full-of-Jesus girl, began going to worldly concerts, dressed all in black, and she didn't enjoy being around her light-reflecting friends any longer.

My heart broke as I watched her relationship with Jesus fade into utter darkness. I interceded and prayed daily for Katy. I knew the only thing that would pull her back into the light would be the power of prayer and for her friendship with Susan to end.

I prayed specific prayers for Katy and Susan. The Scripture tells us in John 14:6 that no one comes to the Father except through Jesus, and Isaiah 10:27 tells us that it is the anointing that breaks the yoke of bondage.

That became my prayer mantra. Bring her heart back to Jesus and break the yoke of bondage in her life. Remove her desire to be a friend of the darkness and bring her back into the light. John 8:12 reminds us that, "Whoever follows me will never walk in darkness, but will have the light of life."

Light and darkness cannot coexist together. It is just like oil and water; they don't mix well together and create utter destruction. Remember, sin is fun for a season, but the end therefore is death. For months I prayed. The harder I prayed, the further Katy went into the world.

Do you ever feel like that? "God, I am doing all I know to do and this situation keeps growing worse. Am I praying wrong? Do

You even hear me? Please help me and show me what to pray, what else to do, and assure me that You are working on this. I need to know You hear me."

It's then that our frustration moves to tears and a broken and contrite spirit moves His heart. The Word I have hidden in my heart rises up and extends hope to me. Even when I don't see it, He is working. Even when I don't feel it, He's working.

I must speak His promises aloud and declare His truths. I am to call those things that are not as though they are. I am to speak to the mountain in front of me and command it to move. I encourage myself in the Lord as I speak faith. The dark clouds then move out of view and the light of His glory shines.

I had to learn that it's great to have verses highlighted in my Bible, but I must have them written on my heart as well. In Psalm 45:1 David said that his tongue was as the pen of a ready writer. The Word states in Proverbs 3:1-3 that we should not forget God's laws but write them on the tablets of our heart.

We see from these two Scriptures that our heart is the tablet and our tongue is the pen. When we confess God's Word aloud, we write it on our own heart, and it becomes more firmly established both in our heart and in the earth.

I never gave up hope on Katy. My heart grieved for Susan as well. One day, just like any other day, I saw Katy. She looked different that day. I saw a glimmer of light return to her eyes. Her language was a bit different and I noticed one HUGE thing. She had color on her clothing.

I didn't say a word, but the Holy Ghost stood up on the inside of me. I heard the Spirit whisper, "She is shifting her heart back to Me. Keep praying, it's working." I wanted to shout at that moment but instead I whispered back a faint, "Thank You, Lord," and kept on keeping on.

A few weeks passed and every time I saw Katy, I noticed a change. A good change. A colorful change. No longer was she dressed all in black with Gothic attire, but this particular day she had on a full-colored pink top. Pink, yes my favorite color, but hot pink; no black lipstick, but a beautiful sheer-pink gloss. You might be thinking, Christi, what does that have to do with anything?

I will tell you that it has to do with EVERYTHING! What we have stored up in our heart reflects to the outside. Proverbs 27:19 reminds us, as water reflects the face, so the heart reflects the person. The light of Jesus was penetrating her heart, therefore it was a direct reflection upon her face. For the first time in months, I saw the Katy that went missing. I watched her transform, and one day she said these words to me, "Did you notice I'm not wearing black anymore?"

I gently smiled and replied, "I noticed the day you added back one piece of color to your wardrobe." I then watched it grow over time. Today, she lives in the light. Instead of Susan influencing her to make bad choices, she loves her from afar. They are still friends but distant. No longer does Katy allow Susan's decisions to dictate her faith.

Katy attends weekly Bible studies with those light-reflecting friends again. She attends her church faithfully, ever growing in the knowledge of truth. When you see someone "going dark," don't ignore it. Reach out to them, pray, and offer a lifeline of hope. You might be the only one that cares enough to save their life.

Remember, when you are full of light, the enemy hates it. He seeks whom he may devour. Don't allow him to dim your light so you won't offend others. Instead make your prayer so bold and ask the Lord to let you shine brighter than the brightest star to reflect His glory.

Next, I want you to meet Gracie. I met Gracie years ago when I was the speaker for a ladies conference. She was on the praise and worship team that hosted the event. Gracie was so beautiful and sang with a great anointing, leading ladies into the throne room. Her personality was precious and I enjoyed her presence. A few years passed and I didn't think about Gracie any longer. At that moment she made a great impact on my life, but like anything else in life, you move on.

It was early one morning as I entered into my prayer closet. Immediately, I saw Gracie's face come into my spirit. I knew that meant I needed to pray for her. I wasn't sure why, but the Spirit never places someone in your mind just because. It is always for a strategic purpose and it's up to us to listen and obey.

When I finished my prayer time, I grabbed my phone and went to her Facebook page to see if she was ok. You know, Facebook is a tell-all, right? Her page popped up and my spirit was instantly grieved. Her profile picture was not the Gracie I knew. She had gone dark. What does that even mean, you might ask? I wasn't looking at Gracie. It was a photo of a sad, depressed, dark soul. Darkness filled her eyes and facial piercings so heavy you could tell it was to try to cover up pain.

Oh, my heart. I knew why the Spirit showed me her face in prayer. She needed a lifeline to pull her back into the light. I instantly sent her a direct message that read:

"Hey sweetie. I have you on my heart today. I feel in my spirit you are struggling and I can't shake it. Talk to me."

Gracie: "Hey, not going to lie. I haven't been doing so great. I'm struggling and satan is attacking me. My family left that church I met you at and we haven't been going anywhere. I miss fellowship and being in God's presence. On top of that I haven't been living 'right' and it has led to many temptations. I miss the close relationship I used to have with God but I just felt I couldn't reach out to anyone."

Do you see how the Lord will disrupt your day to minister to those in need? Gracie needed a lifeline, and if I wasn't in tune with the Spirit, would she still be wandering around in the darkness today?

It is so vitally important to obey the Spirit. When He calls to you and says text so and so, call so and so, pray for so and so, don't delay, pray right away, then reach out. They are waiting on you to draw them back into the light. Because you allowed the Lord to turn you, He is using you.

> Christi: "This is why the Lord won't let me stop thinking of you! Listen to me, you have got to get yourself back in right standing with Jesus. He's coming back any moment for us. You cannot miss the rapture, Gracie. Will you go to church with me Sunday?"

> Gracie: "I will ask my parents if we can. They were going to visit somewhere else but I will definitely ask."

Guess who showed up to church that next Sunday morning? You got it, Gracie, along with her mom and dad. When the altar call was given, all three of them rededicated their lives to the Lord. I held Gracie in my arms like a baby as she wept. Her heart was broken but she found true restoration at the feet of Jesus. So did her parents.

This was well over three years ago and this family is an active part of our church. Gracie even sings on the praise and worship team. The statement holds true: People don't care how much you know until they know how much you care. I cared, therefore I responded.

One thing I have learned in my journey with the Lord is never to be too busy to take notice of someone. We serve an intricate, detailed God. He gives the sparrow a place to lay, so why would we think He doesn't care for our every need? We must keep our spiritual eyes, ears, and hearts open so we can see who waits on us to help them.

One of my favorite songs in this season of life is an oldie but a goodie. It's called "Born to Serve the Lord." My mom has told me from day one that I was born to win souls. I believe that is so true, for my heart longs to see people give their hearts to Jesus. A few of the lyrics in this song are my heart's cry. The verse says, "My hands were made to help my neighbor, my eyes were made to read God's Word, my feet were made to walk in His footsteps, my body is the temple of the Lord."[2]

If we truly are to be the hands and feet of Jesus that reflect His light, then we must notice people in need. We live in such a fast-paced society where people thrive and try to find their worth in their busyness. God didn't call us to be busy. He called us to be fruitful.

You can find yourself so busy doing things for the Lord or even serving in the church that your personal relationship with

---

2 Bud Chambers, "Born to Serve the Lord," Jimmie Davis Music, 1959, 1964.

Jesus suffers. We should never allow that to happen. If it does, we must repent and get back to the main thing being the main thing, which is Jesus at the center of it all.

Remember the story of the Good Samaritan in Luke chapter 10? A man going from Jerusalem to Jericho is attacked by robbers who strip and beat him. A priest and a Levite pass by without helping him. But a Samaritan stops and cares for him and takes him to an inn, where the Samaritan pays for his care. Interesting story, huh?

The ones with the religious titles walked right past him but the Samaritan cared for him. It goes to show you that others may pass you by, but the ones who aren't too busy to care notice.

God is interested in every detail of our lives (Psalm 139:1-4) and knows what we need even before we ask Him (Matthew 6:8). We can approach God's throne of grace with confidence, knowing He will help us in our time of need (Hebrews 4:16).

# Chapter 2

## A GENTLE TURN

Life is like a kaleidoscope. You look through it, twist it a little bit, then with every turn there is a new pattern or color that is highlighted. The inside of a kaleidoscope contains mirrors and pieces of colored glass and shapes whose reflections produce changing patterns when rotated by the viewer. Just as seasons of our lives shift, we must be aware of what turn is made so we can be a continual reflection of His glory.

I am currently in a transition season as I write this chapter. A gentle twist and whisper from the Lord redirected my steps. It is crucial to recognize and obey His voice. If we aren't in proper alignment and are turned a little too far to the world's voice, we could miss a divine turn for the course of our next season.

Daily we should be in the Word of God and study the blueprint for our lives. If He tells us to go left, we go left. If He says right, we go right. I love the Scriptures that begin, "He that hath an ear, let Him hear." That literally means, "Listen up, listen up, I have important things to speak to you. Listen intently to My voice, please."

Proverbs 16:9 states that a man's mind plans his way, but the Lord directs his steps and establishes them. I have had many people tell me they are waiting on the Lord, but He expects us to move our feet. The directions He supplies for us through His Word are crucial.

So many people try to seek a word from the Lord through a prophet, evangelist, etc., when all they need to do is read the Word. You need a word, go read the Word. It's that simple, really.

If you study God's generals in the Bible, all of them were simply in tune with the Spirit. How do you get in tune with the Spirit? By much reading, prayer, fasting, seeking, and intercession in the Spirit. For as many as are led by the Spirit of God, they are the sons of God (Romans 8:14).

Walking in the Spirit is a must if we are to stay in proper alignment. Think on this for a moment…placement is so important. The Lord orders our steps, and if we decide to take that lightly and follow our own steps, we create disaster.

He puts the right people in our life at the right place for the right time. But on the flipside of that, you can put yourself in the wrong place with the wrong people at the wrong time and that never turns out well. God is into details. He loves specifics and intricate things. Even the hair on our head is numbered. He knows us intimately.

When He instructed Noah to build the ark, He had very specific details as to how it was to be built and what was to be put inside the ark. Noah had divine instructions to coat it with pitch inside out. The ark was to be three hundred cubits long, fifty cubits wide, and thirty cubits high.

What if Noah would have said, "I don't want to build it like that? I have a better way I will build this." Do you think Noah and his family would have been saved if he followed his plan instead of the Lord's? I don't think so. You see, they had never even seen rain before. It had never happened, but by faith Noah obeyed the Lord. He followed divine instruction, which led to the saving of his entire family.

Steps are ordered by the Lord. When we say YES to Jesus, guide my steps, we are saying YES to victory. The problem many face is they hear the Lord speaking to them about the twists and the turns but don't like it. They follow their plan instead of God's plan, which typically takes them to a desolate place. Our human reasoning talks us out of the correct spiritual decisions because of logic. When we walk in faith, we don't overthink it. Even if it sounds crazy or doesn't make sense at all, we say, "I'm all in!"

There have been many times in my life when I tried to make a turn myself and it was not God's timing. I tried to force the turn and assist the Lord when frankly, He didn't need my help. When the Lord births something within you, that may not mean to do it within the next five minutes. It might, but typically it begins as a seed and He develops it in you over time.

Back in 2013, I had received a word from the Lord so clearly. I was on a girls trip to celebrate my birthday. My girlfriends and I settled into a hotel room when I had this overwhelming desire to host a ladies conference. The vision was so strong that I immediately put pen to paper and drew out what He was giving me.

I drew a bird soaring in the air with color, design in great detail. He gave me the Scripture Jeremiah 29:13, "When you seek the Lord with your whole heart, you will find Him." I was to call the ladies conference "Seek to Soar" and I would be the keynote speaker. I shared my vision with my girlfriends and we immediately got to work planning and strategizing.

The problem with this wonderful word I received was that I was so excited I didn't really seek the Lord in prayer over it. I just got busy picking a date, music, themes, etc., that were good for my timing and schedule.

Don't ever do that by the way. I should have taken the vision and word, covered it in prayer, and sought Him for the timing. Your flesh gets so excited when you feel something like that, you automatically assume it's a green light to go and don't stop at yellow to even yield. So that's what I did.

Thank the Lord the conference came and went with great anointing, attendance, and blessings, but I learned a lot from it. If I would have waited on the Lord's timing, I wouldn't have had to struggle so hard to pay for it. My ideas were BIG, and even though that's wonderful to Dream Big, I was a one-person ministry in a small beginning. I did get it paid for but with borrowed money and a Holy Ghost spanking from the Lord on listening to Him on timing. If He orders it, He will pay for it. And that's the truth.

I believe we learn from wrong turns. Once we mess up, He twists us back and we can see in clarity what we should have done differently. Our daily walk with the Lord is a journey. Each day we should ever learn in the knowledge of His truth. We are lifetime learners in the school of the Holy Ghost. His Word is our road map that leads us every step of the way.

I once heard a preacher say, "If you aren't as close to the Lord as you once were, who moved? It wasn't Him." That made me think hard about the times in my life that I tried to do it my way or in my timing. My steps got off and as I searched for Him, I found Him right where I left Him.

In life we are going to step out in faith to see if this or that is a right fit for us. Sometimes we will step into something and know immediately that is not what God wants us to do. Other times, we step and it's a perfect fit and we know that it is right.

My grandpa always told me that it's better to step out in faith than to sit down in doubt. If we miss God, He will find us. I loved that because when fear knocks, I knew that it was better step out then sit down.

Doubt, fear, and unbelief block our destiny when we give way to them. When we question if we really heard from God, the enemy is quick to tell us, "No, you didn't." We must not be ignorant of the Word. If we don't know the Word, the enemy will fill us full of lies. "Your Word is a lamp unto my feet and a light unto my path. I have hid Your Word in my heart that I might not sin against You" (Psalm 119:105). When the Word is stored up like a great treasure in our heart, we allow the gentle turn of the Spirit to move us closer to our destiny.

We are carriers of the glory, so the glory should be leading us in all Spirit and truth. Our divine steps, yes, are ordered by the Lord, but we must do our part to fulfill the order. How we carry ourselves is a great reflection of the Kingdom. We should always represent everywhere that we go. When we abide in His presence, people should be able to tell where our time has been spent.

In Exodus 34 the passage tells us of an encounter of the glory. When Moses came down from Mount Sinai he was not aware that his face was radiant because he had been in the presence of the Lord. The glory was so manifested aglow upon Moses that Aaron and the Israelites were afraid to even come near him.

Can you imagine walking into work with your face shining bright like a neon light because you had been in the presence of the Lord? That is just wow. Moses had to keep a veil over his face to the people but would remove it when he went back into the presence of the Lord.

Our goal and desire should be to become so saturated in God's presence that we are truly a daily reflection of His light. If we could ever comprehend what we carry inside of us, we would act differently. Our bodies are the temple of the Holy Ghost and our heart is His home.

Since Jesus abides in our heart and lives there, let me pose some questions to you. Are you keeping your house clean and free from dirt? Are there any impurities that need to be removed? Are you free from bitterness, unforgiveness, strife, and offense? These are a few things to ponder that could cause our reflection to be dim and dark.

We are all lights, some just shine a bit brighter. Maybe if you cleaned your lamp, you would shine brighter too. Have the Word so hidden in your heart that you walk it out in love and strength.

People watch your life. Whether you believe it or not, they do. Social media is the newest way to represent or to show the world who and what we are about. Your page asks for a profile picture, a short biography of who you are, etc. That page is a reflection of who you truly are. If you want to know if someone is true blue, go read their Facebook page. It's a tell-all to their most innermost thoughts and opinions. I just clicked on Facebook as I write this to see what the latest update asks. It simply says, "What is on your mind?"

That is a loaded question, if you ask me. Whew, do we really want to know what is on the mind of someone? I don't think we probably do, but Facebook, Instagram, etc., are wonderful ways to represent and reflect. When someone sees me, I pray they see and say, "Oh yes, Christi Johnston is a woman of God who reflects Christ well." I would never want people to say my name and attach it to gossip, slander, etc. We must represent our King!

Let me share a neat story with you on representation. It was 2011 and I just wrote my first book about our special-needs daughter. It was the story of our faith journey. I received a phone call and was asked to come share our story at a Rotary Club meeting. Strange I know, but through a family connection, I was asked. I accepted but hesitantly, knowing I had no clue what I was doing. I walked into a very fancy country club where the meeting was being held. As I gazed upon the expensive chandeliers, I felt so out of place. *What am I doing here?*

I made my way into the corridor as a gentleman met and greeted me. He told me to make myself comfortable and he would be right back. I stood there frozen and thought, *Who am I and what on earth am I doing here?* Truth be told, I wanted to run out the door and hide, but I had committed, so I had to proceed.

I walked over to the table that held all the name badges that the people would place upon them as they entered the meeting. It was the metal name badges with the magnet that would hold it onto the shirt. The fancy kind, ya know.

I started at the top and read down the list of badges. The more I read the more I shook. No one informed me this was an all-MAN meeting and I was the only WOMAN. The badges were of people with professions like this: doctor; CEO of a national bank; lawyer; a specialist in neuroscience; CEO of a health organization.

Are you catching the drift yet? I was in pure panic. I could not believe that I was the one that was about to get up and speak to these elite men. I was beyond intimidated, scared, and to be honest, I felt I could vomit, LOL! I took in all the names and information, then stood in disbelief.

I simply spoke these words in my mind, *Jesus, You have to help me right now. I cannot do this. I am Christi Johnston, vo tech, eleven months.* Seriously, that is all I could think. As soon as I said that, the Lord gave me a vision. I looked back at the table and at the very bottom I saw a badge that was not there before. In the spirit realm I saw a badge with my name on it. It read this: Christi Johnston, Ambassador of the Lord Jesus Christ.

I couldn't believe my eyes. I looked, then looked off then back again. Sure enough, the Lord placed it there just for me. In my spirit I picked it up, placed it on, and pulled my shoulders back.

A very strong anointing suddenly came upon me as I knew who I was. I was sent there by the Lord to reflect His light. I was His personal representative chosen to share my story for His glory.

As the men filed into the room, I stood there confident in my representation. I took the podium, shared from my heart, and all I can say is it was all God, because I was so not confident in myself, but He filled my mouth with goodness. As a matter of fact, as I spoke a doctor stood up and said these words, "I like this story. I want to give you $100."

Everyone laughed and clapped. I was in shock that he wanted to give me money, but I know it was the Holy Ghost he felt. It moved him and he didn't have a clue what to do with it.

I'm telling you it was an experience I will never forget. That day I truly learned what an ambassador was. "Therefore, we are ambassadors for Christ, God making his appeal through us. We implore you on behalf of Christ, be reconciled to God" (2 Corinthians 5:20, ESV).

That day could have turned out so differently if I wouldn't have called upon His name to help me. He is a very present help in the time of trouble. Just the mention of His name changes things. There is no other name given among men whereby we must be saved. All power is in the name of Jesus. "And whatever you do in word or deed, do all in the name of the Lord Jesus, giving thanks to God the Father through Him" (Colossians 3:17, NKJV).

Since that experience, I have had hundreds, probably thousands more encounters. Once I figured out who I was, I ran with Jesus and never looked back. I had to face fear, anxiety, and rejection, but each time I faced it head-on, He stood with me and gave me strength.

I have found that people appreciate your strengths but relate better with your weaknesses. Authenticity is missing in today's society. All the highlight reels, the posting "your best" days are so deceiving. I once posted a lowlight reel of my week just to let people in on my life. I can promise you it's far from glamorous.

Being special-needs parents brings so many challenges. I have dedicated the last twenty years to sharing our story to bring God the glory. Our trials have only made us stronger. I believe a reflection of light and hope is on display for the world to see through my family. Even when circumstances are awful and we don't understand, I can declare, "God is still good."

We encounter frustrated faith, but the good Lord gave us feelings for a reason. He understands my frustrations and holds me when I cry. My oldest daughter Meg said Hannah is the trial that built her. To me that was a profound statement.

Having a sibling with special needs is not for the faint of heart. It is tough. But look at the strength and tenacity Meg has earned through this hardship. I can say without a doubt that this trial has made my family stronger. We chose to run to God, not from Him, when our world shattered.

Luke 9:23 states, "If any man will come after me, let him deny himself, and take up his cross daily and follow me" (KJV). Those are Jesus' words directly in red. He tells us we have a daily choice to do this. Not just on Sundays or Wednesdays, but daily deny our flesh to follow Him. I like to say you can't live on yesterday's blessings.

It's a new day. A day full of new grace and mercy that waits upon each of us. I don't know about you, but I run out quickly some days and I am oh so thankful He has a whole new batch whipped up for me the next day. I'm definitely not perfect in my behavior, but it is my heart's desire to be.

As we allow the Lord to turn us each day, we should ask these questions: Do I reflect Him well? Is He proud of me? Do my words give life to others? Do I draw others to the light or push them farther away?

The Word of God is a mirror for our soul. We should look into it to see what our reflection portrays. If you want to know if you are doing well, just listen to your words, for out of the abundance of the heart the mouth speaks.

"Careful, little eyes, what you see. Careful, little ears, what you hear. Careful, little mouth, what you speak." You remember that little song? It makes much more sense to me as an adult. As a child, I didn't understand the relevance to that cute little song. Now I do. It takes on an entirely new meaning to me.

Even as I write this, I am doing a heart check on myself. Search me and know me, O God. Create in me a clean heart and a right spirit. If I have done anything to sin against You, forgive me. Turn me, turn me, turn me as a reflection of Your light. May the words of my mouth and the meditation of my heart be pure before You. When the world sees me, let them see You. Christ in me, the hope of glory!

If you a follow me, then you will follow Him. I have people tell me daily, "Oh, I follow you on social media. I'm just seeing what you are up to." Some follow just to be nosy, but others truly follow me because I follow Jesus.

We must lead by example in our daily lives as well as what we post and portray on social media. I can't help but think if the disciples would have had social media back then what the posts would be like. I just made myself laugh, to be honest.

You know you can say all day long that no one follows you, but oh they do. Maybe not on social media, but parents, your children follow you. What you do, they do. You teach them daily to pursue Christ or the world. It's vitally important that you train them up in the fear and admonition of the Lord. If you don't teach about Jesus, the world will teach them all the wrong things.

Fill them up daily with the love of Jesus. Read the Word with them. Take them to church and talk about the things of the Lord in your homes. Parents, now more than ever we need you to RE-FLECT the hope and light of Jesus Christ. The enemy seeks whom he may devour.

I can promise you that if you allow your child to become vulnerable to anything and everything this world offers, the end of that is destruction. Don't play around with darkness, for dark and the light cannot and will not dwell together.

As I type this I feel such an urgency in my spirit to warn you about handing phones, computers, tablets, etc., to your kids. Don't do it! Monitor everything they watch, because one wrong click can turn into a lifetime addiction, later on to sin. It's truly the bait of satan as he uses anything he can to get into the hearts and minds of the children. It is our job to protect our children. Cover them daily in prayer and plead the blood of Jesus over them. They need your covering!

Prayer is the most powerful tool we have. Prayers go where we can't. I can assure you that the prayers of my parents and grandparents are the reason I am saved today. Train up a child in the way they should go and when they are old they won't depart from it. They can try to run from the Lord but your anointed prayers will chase them down. You absolutely cannot outrun a mother's prayer.

I believe if we understood how powerful prayer is, we would pray more than ever. I am guilty myself of saying, "Well, all we can do is pray," after I've exhausted all my resources to try to fix a problem.

Prayer should be our first thought, not our last resort. The enemy knows if he can get us to have a weak, watered-down prayer life, we become vulnerable to his tactics. We must have the Word hidden in our heart and use it to send him to flight, in Jesus' name. The Word is our weapon that destroys every evil work of the enemy.

We all need to walk in the Word. We are the temple of the Holy Ghost. When we have the fullness of the Lord inside, it's as the old song says, "Jesus on the inside, working on the outside, oh what a change in me." Our goal in life should be to shine so bright that others ask what it is that we have.

I have always said I wanted to be so full of Jesus that He spills out onto everyone around me. When we spend time in His presence we can't help but desire more and more and more. Truly what we pursue is our passion. A passionate pursuit should be all of our heart's desire. We make time for what is important to us. The Lord deserves our firstfruits, not our leftovers. The best of us, not the rest of us!

We make time for what is important to us. In the day and hour in which we live, we are too busy. Instant gratification satisfies the flesh, which leads us to desire more of the ME mentality. Our adversary, the enemy, is the master manipulator. His primary goal is to get us distracted so we lose our focus. We must make it a priority to keep our eyes on the main thing, which is Jesus.

We are warned in 1 Peter 5:8 that satan is like a roaring lion, seeking whom he may devour. His eyes are roaming to and fro, waiting for an opportunity to pounce on us in our weakest moment. This is why it is so incredibly important to know the Word of God. When the enemy attacks, you use the Word as your weapon. At the name of Jesus, he has to flee.

Many people have Scriptures highlighted but that will not be good enough when the attack comes. The Word must be written upon your heart, hidden, and then used to send the enemy to flight. He does not have power or authority over you, for Jesus gave us ALL power and authority over the enemy. Satan lost his, so he wants to take yours.

A no-trespassing sign should be posted by the Spirit so he cannot access you. Get out the purple paint and mark your territory. Stop allowing him to have free rein on your land. As a child of the Most High King, you have Kingdom rights.

Accessibility to you should not be easy, for the Holy King abides in your heart. The enemy can roar, pounce, growl, and seek, but he cannot access or defeat you unless you give him permission.

I have found when people say they are "under attack" all the time it's because they have never learned to be "on the attack."

You must get a holy growl in your belly and become like a pit bull in the Spirit, and use the Word as your weapon. Take up that welcome mat that is at your front door. Not everyone is welcome to enter. Satan, you are not welcome in my home, my heart, my mind, nor my family. Get thee behind, in Jesus' mighty name.

I truly believe when you rise up in boldness and take your authority in Christ, you have reached a new level. The turn that happens when that occurs opens you up for new territory in the Spirit. Sometimes it's not a "gentle turn" but a hard shift to the right when the Spirit says to move.

I heard a saying that made me laugh that goes along with this. The gentleman shared that sometimes the Lord speaks through a whisper, a gentle one, sometimes a roar, or simply a two-by-four. You get to choose which one to listen to. I mean really, I don't want to have to get hit over the head by a two-by-four, but He will do whatever it takes to get our attention. If He doesn't have our full attention, He will disturb what does. Think about it.

I want to question you, the reader, at this moment. Stop and ponder these momentarily. What has your utmost attention? Where does your mind wander off to the most? If you look at your bank account, where does most of your money go? These questions will answer where your passion is. "For where your treasure is, there your heart will be also" (Matthew 6:21, KJV).

# Chapter 3

## MIRRORS

If you have ever looked into a kaleidoscope you notice the reflecting mirrors tilted to each other at an angle. Typically, these mirrors are in a symmetrical pattern when viewed from the end. These reflectors are enclosed in a tube that contains a cell with loose, colored pieces of glass to be reflected in a pattern. Its rotating pattern brings so much uniqueness to the eye. By rotating the mirrors you get unlimited views of changing lights, colors, and various shapes. Isn't that just like us?

As humans, God created us in all shapes, sizes, and colors. There are no two people exactly alike on this earth. Down to our fingerprints, the uniqueness is profound. "For you created my inmost being, you knit me together in my mother's womb" (Psalm 139:13, NIV). Before I was, You already had me created as You wanted me to be. My color, my size, and my shape; You gave me life. I may have not been planned by my parents, but You had a great purpose for me. Your plans are always perfect!

The Lord gives us the spiritual mirror of His Word, the Bible, so we can see who we are and how He sees us. He reminds us that He created us in His image (Genesis 1:27). The Word also shows us who we really are. Our sinful hearts must be exposed to the mirror of His truth to change us.

Change is something we all struggle with. I hear people say all the time, "Well, I was born this way, no changing me." That's just what they want to say because they fear change. How can you reflect the light of Christ daily when you never grow or change? Your light will dim without change and growth. You have heard the phrase, "Nothing changes if nothing changes." It's true. If we want to grow we must face the fear of change head-on.

I love to write and place affirmations on my mirror. When I get ready in the morning, I have the Word of God on my mirror. I can say the Scriptures aloud and declare the works of the Lord. When I speak who I am, I see myself as He sees me. I am fearfully and wonderfully made in His perfect image.

In the last book I wrote I shared so much on our identity in Christ. Even though this is three years later, it's still an area that people struggle with daily. One thing I can tell you for sure is that comparing yourself to others is one of the enemy's greatest tools.

Social media is like a huge mirror of the world that sucks people in at such a fast pace. You see people with bigger houses, nicer cars, all the highlight reels of their "perfect" life but never the lowlight reels. That is how the enemy plants a seed in your head.

You then look in the mirror and see yourself as less than. This is why it is so very important to allow the Word of God to be your mirror. With a biblical worldview, you see with supernatural eyes. With a carnal worldview, you see with worldly eyes.

The Word talks about the three gates. What you let in your heart through your eye and ear gate will exit through your mouth gate. This is why Solomon warned us to guard our hearts with all vigilance, for out of the abundance of the heart the mouth speaks. We guard our hearts by taking care of what we allow to enter into it.

If we monitor what comes into our minds by what we listen to, read, and watch, then we are less likely to be ashamed of what comes out of our mouths. You absolutely cannot take in daily trash and reflect the light! If you want to be a blessing to others and mirror truth, "Guard your gates." Read the Word, pray, fast, and meditate on the goodness of God.

My oldest daughter shared a story with me and I feel it appropriate to share it now. Meg was raised in church, has a personal relationship with Jesus, and pursues holiness. She had started watching a TV series that was interesting. At first she really loved it and couldn't wait to watch the next one. Little by little she told me that she could feel the Spirit convict her about what she was watching. There were various things in the series that she knew wasn't pleasing to the Lord.

She decided to quit watching the series in obedience to the Lord. One day she was cleaning her house and stubbed her toe or something like that. At that moment a curse word came into her mind to yell out. Immediately she recognized that and thought, *Why did that even come into my mind? I don't even cuss and never have.* Instantly the Spirit spoke to her and said, "It was those shows you were watching. You were hearing it, therefore it got into your spirit." Her gates had become unguarded. You see how the enemy works?

There are several points I want to state here:

- I am thankful that the Holy Ghost leads, guides, and convicts us. The Holy Ghost is your best friend. If you don't feel convicted when you do or watch something that doesn't glorify the Lord, check yourself.

- Do not allow things to be easily accessible to enter into your gates. Protect your anointing.

- Watch your circle carefully. We tend to become who we hang around. Make sure your circle chases Jesus, not worldly pursuits.

- If everyone else does it, run the other way.

- We are a separated people called unto holiness. We should not act, talk, walk, or look like the world. We were born to reflect HIS LIGHT!

- Stop following the crowd. They are lost.

Everything we do should be a reflection of what we have stored up in our heart. If you could take a selfie of your soul, would it be beautiful enough to post? Think on that. What is stored up in your heart? Bitterness, strife, anger; love, joy, goodness. If you want to be healthy, check those areas first, then you can concentrate on everything else later.

I really hope I am conveying how important it is to keep a repentant heart. When we repent, we make an about-face and turn the opposite way. We ask Jesus to forgive us of our sins, cleanse our hearts, and keep it free of anything contrary to the Word.

This is something we must do daily. We can't just repent at church on Sundays but daily. Jesus told His disciples in Matthew 16:24, "Whoever wants to be My disciple must deny themselves and take up their cross and follow Me." This calls for full submission in pursuit of our King.

Remember that saying, "Mirror, mirror on the wall"? It comes from a Snow White movie where the evil queen had a mirror that would reveal the answers to her questions. Every day she would ask the mirror, "Mirror, mirror on the wall, who's the fairest of them all?" The mirror would answer, "Thou, O Queen, art the fairest in the land." But one fine day, it answered, "Snow White, O Queen, is the fairest of them all." This is what leads to the queen's plot to murder Snow White to reclaim her place as the fairest maiden in the land. Can you see the analogy here of how the mirror lied to her but then the truth prevailed?

I can't help but use a spiritual analogy here. If you were to look in the mirror today and ask the question, "Mirror, mirror on the wall, who's the fairest of them all?" would you be deceived by the enemy's voice or would you be able to distinguish the voice of truth?

The enemy knows the truth well. We better know the truth well so we can discern his lies. He is a master manipulator and the father of all lies. He has never told the truth and never will.

When we truly have the revelation of our identity being in Christ, we not only see our value but others see it as well. I heard a story once that peach trees don't go around waving their limbs shouting, "Hey, I'm a peach tree." They just grow peaches and everyone knows them by the fruit they produce. Same for us, we bear good fruit, producing the love of Jesus, which draws others to the light.

We reflect the glory daily. We don't have to shout that we are Christians because our lives reflect it. When you get up in the morning, look in the mirror and declare His Word over your life. Speak the Word over yourself until it becomes alive in your heart.

Nothing irritates the enemy more than a Christian who truly knows their worth and value in Christ. When you know that you know, you are a blood-bought child of God. He cannot stand it! Declare it out of your mouth and watch His promises come to life over you.

In this season I hear the Lord speaking on proper alignment. We are the bride of Christ, therefore we must be in position to move forward in battle. When we move, others move. The body of Christ works together in unity to overcome the darkness. It's high time the light of His glory be shed abroad to the nations.

Yes, we should daily represent, but the Lord calls us to move out beyond the four walls of the church. We must have boots on the ground, walking, talking, and carrying the Gospel to a lost and dying world.

Our active duty is to store up the Word of God in our heart and carry it out to the highways and byways. There is no greater calling in life than the calling of soul winning. If you are a born-again believer, then you are called to shine and reflect the light. Jesus didn't give us His glorious Spirit to sit down and keep it hidden. We are a lighthouse to the world.

> "You are the light of the world. A city situated on a hill cannot be hidden. No one lights a lamp and puts it under a basket, but rather on a lampstand, and gives it light to all that are in the house. In the same way let your light shine before others, so that they may see your good works and give glory to your Father in heaven" (Matthew 5:14-16, CSB).

I feel the Spirit saying, "It is time to shine! No more hiding in fear, anxiety, or the 'I'm not good enough to be used' talk. You are more than anointed and equipped for this hour." The mirror that looks back at you should encourage you—not discourage you. We know it's the mirror of His Word that we must look into. The mirror of self will cause us to see every blemish, fault, and unworthy trait, but we look to the Word for our true reaction.

The enemy loves to make us feel like we are not good enough or we don't know enough Scripture to share the Gospel with others. This is why we cannot be moved by our feelings but must be moved by the Word of the Lord.

Feelings are fickle. They will tell us that everyone sees the dark places of our life, which may cause us not to share our testimony. I need to remind you that we are made overcomers by the blood of the Lamb and by the word of our testimony. That's what the Bible tells us. We must share our story for His glory. Our mess is a message of hope to a dark world.

We all have a story to tell. It's our own personal story and no one else has it. Some of you will reach people that I can't. My circle of influence looks totally different than some of yours. Thankfully, I was raised in a godly Christian home, so I can't relate with someone coming out of addiction. But someone reading this book can. Your story of rescue, recovery, and restoration can lead the masses into salvation.

As the light grows inside of you, you share your testimony. The darkness that once enslaved you no longer has any authority over you. Shout it to the world, that your Jesus is a deliverer!

"For when you were slaves of sin, you were free with regard to righteousness. So what fruit was produced then from the things you are now ashamed of? The outcome of those things is death. But now, since you have been set free from sin and have become enslaved to God, you have your fruit, which results in sanctification—and the outcome is eternal life! For the wages of sin is death, but the gift of God is eternal life in Christ Jesus our Lord" (Romans 6:20-23, CSB).

This passage clearly tells us that the darkness had you bound but now the light has come and gives you the blessed hope of eternal life. Your life is truly a message for the world to see. When others see what the Lord has done for you, it gives hope.

So many people think they are too far gone. The master deceiver has blinded them, but it is our job as children of the Lord to tell them there is a blessed hope! God is no respecter of persons; what He does for one, He will do for another. It's level ground around Calvary. He truly loves us all. His death, burial, and resurrection were for you and for me. Because of His shed blood on Calvary we can be saved.

I read the book, *The Prophetic Warrior,* by Emma Stark. This book challenged me in multiple ways and pulled me out of my comfort zone. She shared a personal story of how the Lord used her while she was shoe shopping. I can hear some of you now, "Oh, that makes me a nervous wreck." Yeah, me too. But when the Lord tells you to do something, we must obey.

She spoke to the lady that rang up her shoes. She told her that her name was Emma and she was a prophet who hears from God. Of course, the lady was stunned, as I would be too. I have never heard anyone announce themselves in such a fashion.

Here's the part that was so interesting to me. Emma said, "How will anyone make a withdrawal from you if they don't know what you carry?"

The lady replied, "Well, what does He say about me?"

Emma replied, "The Lord says you are going to be a good mom."

Immediately the young lady began to cry. Through her tears she blurted out that she had just found out that morning that she was pregnant. She hadn't told a soul, not even her boyfriend. She already had an appointment booked for an abortion on Thursday of that week. That same morning she prayed for the first time and said this, "God, if You are real, would You please tell me what to do about this pregnancy?" Then she looked up at Emma and said, "If God says I am going to be a good mom, I am canceling my abortion."

Did that send chills all over your body like it did mine? When I read that, I knew Emma had understood the assignment clearly and was in tune with the Spirit.

You never know how, when, or where the Lord will use you, but we must always be ready. Scripture states to be instant in season and out. That means to always be ready to share at any time!

Do you think Emma had a clue that day while out shoe shopping that her obedience would change the trajectory of someone else's life? Not just one life but two! That unborn baby would now live all because Emma shared a word the Lord had given her.

I want to challenge you with this story. You may not be an actual prophet in your gifting, but you most definitely can hear from the Lord as He directs you. Jesus wants us all to be brave, bold, and a shining light! This story is proof that He uses people to do His work.

Our job is just to be obedient and share even when we are uncomfortable. I would much rather step out and miss it then not obey. That is how we learn and grow our faith. The next time you look in the mirror, make some declarations aloud:

- I am strong, brave, and bold (2 Corinthians 12:9-10).
- I speak the promises of God that are yes and amen (2 Corinthians 1:20).
- I have the Holy Ghost living on the inside of me that gives me peace, comfort, and strength (1 Corinthians 3:16).

- I am the head and not the tail, above and not beneath (Deuteronomy 28:13).

- I can do all things through Christ who strengthens me (Philippians 4:13).

- I am blessed coming in and going out (Deuteronomy 28:6).

- God has not given me the spirit of fear but of power, love, and a sound mind (2 Timothy 1:7).

- By His stripes I am healed (1 Peter 2:24).

- I am a new creature in Christ Jesus (2 Corinthians 5:17).

- Greater is He who is in me than he who is in the world (1 John 4:4).

- I walk by faith and not by sight (2 Corinthians 5:7).

- No weapon formed against me shall prosper (Isaiah 54:17).

- My God supplies all my needs according to His riches in glory (Philippians 4:19).

- I live under God's supernatural protection (Psalm 91:1-2).

- God has great plans for me and I am filled with hope for a great future (Jeremiah 29:11).

# Chapter 4

## I'LL SAY YES, LORD, YES

I remember in 1998 when this chorus became a mantra in my life. I am singing it aloud as this chapter unfolds.

> *I'll say, "Yes, Lord, yes"*
> *To Your will and to Your way*
> *I'll say, "Yes, Lord, yes"*
> *I will trust You and obey*
> *When the Spirit speaks to me*
> *With my whole heart I'll agree*
> *And my answer will be, "Yes, Lord, yes"*[3]

I prayed this daily when I was a babe in Christ. My heart was pliable and ready for use. Anything He asked me to do I was saying, "Yes, Lord, yes. I am available." I would witness to anyone at any time. There was nothing in me that was embarrassed or afraid. My passionate pursuit for Jesus was on display for the world to see.

---

[3] Lynn Keesecker, "Yes, Lord, Yes" © 1983 by Manna Music Inc.

I remember counting down the days and the hours for our home Bible studies. I couldn't wait to get to the prayer room. I never missed a church service, for I knew my King would meet me there. I went with expectancy and knew as the praises went up, the glory came down.

This is the year I totally surrendered every part of me to Jesus. As a child, I was raised in church but I was so little, I truly don't remember a whole lot of it. I went to church because my parents told me we were going. As I got older my parents didn't take us as much and I got out of the habit of going.

I never even thought about Jesus nor did I go to church for many years. That all changed when I met a cute boy whose parents were devout Christians, and as long as he lived under their roof, that boy would be at church. Well guess what? What better way to see your boyfriend than to go to church with him?

Lame excuse, I know, but dating Jamie is how I found myself back in a church house. Up until then I had religion—not relationship. Once I found a personal relationship with Jesus, everything changed, and I mean everything. My passions, desires, the way I carried myself, all began to truly reflect His light. Through study of His Word, He began to navigate my life. He was the captain of my ship and I said, "Yes, Lord, yes. Whatever You ask: YES!"

I am a hairstylist by trade and my newfound passion was on display behind the chair. This is the WHY behind this book, to allow the Lord to use you where you are at. You can reflect His light in all you do. My clients noticed a big change in me, which prompted the question, "What happened to you? You seem so happy and fulfilled. Tell me more."

This is where the "Revival Hub" began to happen. Whew, I am about to shout as I type this. As I think back to this time, my spirit is renewed as I share this. My clients and my coworkers felt the overflow of the Living Water that was inside of me.

I would do a haircut and then have so many opportunities to share the Gospel with them. Some came to the Lord for the first time, right there in my salon chair. Others wept as we prayed for healing over medical issues, lost family, etc. As all of this happened, lives were transformed by His Spirit, all because of my YES.

Do you see how the Lord uses us if we are simply available? This is a good place to remind you, the reader, that God doesn't look for abilities, just availability! Your YES can mean salvation for others. We are to be so full of Jesus that it overflows onto our neighbors.

This is so true for me. I am not exaggerating when I tell you that our salon became a "Revival Hub." My parents owned the salon, so we could have church whenever we wanted! The years of 1998-2005 were years of the Holy Ghost and fire. We had so many people hungry for the Lord, for real, that we made a sign and put on the back room of the salon that said, "Upper Room."

I am laughing as I type this. It was truly unbelievable. People were getting saved, healed, and filled, all at a one-stop shop—the hair salon. Several times we prayed with someone that ended up at the church and were water baptized. The old man was dead and the new man was resurrected with Christ. Most of them would be filled with the Holy Ghost with the evidence of speaking in other tongues. Truly this was a time of epic revival. I honestly cannot even tell you how many lives were forever changed.

One story I want to share with you is just wow. That's truly the only way I know how to explain what happened with this coworker of mine. This was at the time 9/11 happened. It was the year of 2001, the world was chaotic. I will never forget this particular day. I had my own room where I cut hair off the front of the waiting area. This young lady I worked with came running to my room. She was weeping as she cried out, "Christi, I don't want to go to hell. I'm so afraid! Is this the end of the world? Help me, I need to know Jesus."

I grabbed her and held her like a mother would a child. I then lead her in a prayer of repentance as she cried out to Jesus. Her heart was so tender as she made a decision that day to follow Him.

Later that day, we had a break in between clients. The two of us decided to make a Sonic run for a Coke. We chatted about Jesus and I told her that the Holy Ghost was still all over her. As I drove to Sonic, in my car she prayed again. Then out of nowhere she started to speak in tongues. You have to understand, this girl, didn't even know the story of Adam and Eve. She tried to ask me what was happening to her but nothing would come out but tongues.

Y'all, I have never seen anything like this in my life. She could not speak in English. This went on for hours, no exaggeration. She tried to order a Dr Pepper at Sonic and it came out in tongues. I laughed so hard, I couldn't breathe. The spirit of joy filled my car, which allow us both to pray in tongues. What an encounter she had! Scripture tells us that He fills and feeds the hungry.

You can only imagine how this flowed all over the rest of the salon. We would all laugh for days on end as we watched her be transformed by the power of the Spirit. My, oh my, the stories I have to tell. We all have a testimony to share. Our willingness to say yes to the Lord is a game changer.

Our fruit will do the talking. Our life mission is to walk in love, pull others up higher, and reflect the glory. It's all about souls.

If we aren't concerned about the salvation of others, something is badly wrong with us. As a born-again believer, not only should we keep our hearts pure and holy before the Lord, but we should always be ready to help lead others. The Jesus in us should shine so bright that others are drawn in.

I heard a saying once that is really funny but true, "If you have Jesus in your heart, make sure you notify your face," LOL! Sour

Suzys are not a great draw for the Kingdom and neither are Negative Nancys. Walking in love while sharing the goodness of God is of upmost importance.

So many opportunities are presented to us daily to spread the good news of the Gospel. It doesn't matter where we are at, if we say yes to the Lord, He will use us. One thing that will help each of us to be bold in our walk is to stay full of His Spirit. Our daily reading and prayer time equip us to conquer each day.

Scripture tells us that we are to walk in the Spirit. That doesn't mean that we walk around on a glory cloud 24/7, but we are in the mind of the Spirit. We keep our mind and our heart set upon Jesus. No matter what we have going on, our affections are focused on Him.

In Matthew 28:16-20 we read about the Great Commission. Jesus calls on His followers to make disciples and baptize them.

- He commands us to preach the Gospel to all nations and people.
- Work miracles in Jesus' name to testify to the Gospel.
- Baptize new believers.
- Disciple those who receive Christ.

After someone gives their life to the Lord, they must get discipled. Every person needs a mentor in their life. Someone who will take them under their wing to lead and guide them in their future steps.

I preached a sermon once called "Add On" and I truly believe this is a message every believer needs to hear. Too many people stay in the infancy stage of their walk in Christ and never add on. We are to be lifetime learners that continue to grow in the knowledge of the truth.

Once we have made a personal commitment to follow Jesus, we need to add on. Daily we should ask the Lord, "What can I add on next?" Whether it be water baptism, infilling of the Holy Ghost, or gifts of the Spirit, there is always more. This year our heart's cry should be more of Jesus, less of me.

In Matthew 16:24, Jesus told His disciples, "Whoever wants to be my disciple must deny themselves and take up their cross and follow me" (NIV). Jesus asked His followers if they were willing to follow Him to their death. To die to self. To sacrifice their own personal ambitions, dreams, and expectations. He asked His disciples if they would take up their cross of self-denial and self-surrender.

In addition to serving others, to take up your cross involves living a life that imitates Christ's example. This means living a life of humility, compassion, and forgiveness. We must be willing to put aside our own pride and prioritize the needs of others, just as Christ did when He washed the feet of His disciples.

The society we currently live in is the polar opposite of this. People are full of pride, self, and all about, what is in it for me? Instead of serving others they want to be served. It's a sad reality, but the truth of the matter is that Scripture is being fulfilled. Second Timothy 3:2-5 states, "For people will only love themselves and their money. They will be boastful and proud, scoffing at God, disobedient to parents, and ungrateful" (NLT).

Look around…it is at every hand. If only every born-again believer would truly surrender it all to the Lord, the world would be a different place. When I focus on my own personal problems, I get overwhelmed. I then shift my focus on blessing others. A servant's heart seeks to love as Christ loved us. Through service, we manifest God's love and grace, and show the transformative power of His love (Galatians 5:13).

There are three essential ingredients for developing a servant's heart:

- Humility. True humility involves an honest assessment of our strengths and weaknesses.
- Sacrifice, meeting the needs of others.
- Faith. God never asks us to separate the concepts of service and reward. "Behold my servant whom I uphold" (Isaiah 42:1, ESV).

The Lord is the One who should uphold us at all times. Living to serve is the love walk that we are called into. Scripture after Scripture tells us to be devoted to one another in love, honoring one another above ourselves. The words love and serve are dependent upon each other. To love is to serve. To love on someone else is to put their joy before your own. To serve is the paramount way to display love.

Jesus was the ultimate servant who showed compassion in all He displayed, washing the feet of His disciples, His love and concern for the sick and the oppressed, etc. Jesus described Himself as a servant when He said, "The Son of Man did not come to be served, but to serve" (Mark 10:45, NIV). He modeled servanthood when He came to dwell among us as a man who obeyed God's will.

Here are a few ways you can love and serve your neighbor and reflect His glory:

- Pray blessings upon them daily.
- Let them know you are there for them by giving of your time.
- Be a good listener.
- Bless them with a warm meal just because you love them.
- Assist with a need if applicable: a ride, checking on their home while they are on vacation, feeding their animals, etc.

When we say YES to Jesus, everything changes. We become the moldable clay in the Potter's hand that is ready for use. The key to Kingdom building is serving. If you see a need, don't wait for someone else to do it. If it is possible for you to do it, you fulfill the need. Too many times we wait for someone else to do it. When Jesus says, "You do it," you say, "YES!"

The busyness of our society is sickening, to be honest. The busier we are, the more accomplished we feel. I know people that are workaholics that feel like they are sinning if they are not working. That is not the design or the plan Jesus laid out for us. We will discuss rest in another chapter, but the *busier-the-better* concept is not all it's cracked up to be.

I once heard an evangelist state that being busy meant "being under satan's yoke." Boy, did that ever make my spirit jump. I never want to be under his yoke, nor do I want to be so busy that I can't sit at my Master's feet. You have heard the term, if the devil can't make you bad, he will make you busy, right? He wants us to be so busy that we forget to spend time with the Lord. He knows if he can get us distracted, offended, or isolated that he can whisper into our ears. I can just see that liar, grasping his hands, hoping we give him a listening ear. As he whispers lies, our spirit must be filled with truth.

How can we know if the enemy is lying to us if we don't know the Word? Think about that for a minute. There is a reason we must have the Word hidden so deeply in our heart. Busyness leads to distraction and distraction leads to a shallow love walk. If our love walk is shallow, we cannot fulfill the Scriptures. If we are always too busy to serve someone in need, how can the Lord trust us and use us?

I never want the Lord to say to me, "I wish you wouldn't have been so busy with things that weren't advancing the Kingdom. I could have used you greatly, Christi, but you were too busy for Me."

It reminds me of the Scripture in Matthew 7:21-23, "Not everyone who says to me, 'Lord, Lord,' will enter into the kingdom of heaven, but only the one who does the will of my Father who is in heaven. Many will say to me on that day, 'Lord, Lord, did we not prophesy in your name and in your name drive out demons and in your name drive out demons and in your name perform many miracles?' Then I will tell them plainly, 'Depart from me you worker of iniquity, I never knew you' " (CSB).

That verse shakes me to my core. If it doesn't you, I would stop right now and do a heart check.

- Is my heart pure and holy before You, Lord?
- I repent for anything that would distract me from Your presence that causes me to be too busy.
- Search me and know me; wash me clean and purify my heart.
- Don't allow me to be deceived by having a form of godliness but denying the power thereof.
- I want to hear You say: "Well done, thou good and faithful servant, enter thou in."

I want to simply say, "Yes, Lord, yes," for all You ask of me.

In closing of this chapter I want to share a few personal stories to build your faith.

Many years ago I was driving to Bible study on a Wednesday night. It was just a normal drive until I got past a double bridge. I saw something out of the corner of my eye moving under the bridge but didn't give it a second thought. You know I was BUSY and on my way to church. I didn't have time to notice someone in need because I have a schedule, right? Wrong.

I heard the gentle voice of my King whisper into my ear as soon as I passed the bridges. He spoke, "Turn around, go to her." I thought, Oh Lord, do I have to? Honest truth, it felt like my car stopped and turned itself around.

The heart of Jesus pulled my car around and His compassion moved through me. I got out of my vehicle terrified but saying aloud, "The Lord does not give me the spirit of fear but of power, love, and a sound mind." I kept quoting Scriptures to calm me as I approached a sad, tortured, lonely young lady curled up in a ball underneath the bridge. I could tell she was under the influence of who knows what but as I got closer to her, I felt a calming peace come over me.

I sat down right beside her and asked her name. She told me and I told her mine. I asked her why she was under the bridge and she told me she didn't have anywhere else to go. She was very confused and afraid. I scooted super close to her and asked if I could hug her. She let me and then fell apart in my arms. I sat under that bridge holding a hopeless woman while I spoke hope into her. I prayed over her and she prayed with me.

After we talked a while, I asked her if there was anywhere I could take her to get out of the cold. By this time she seemed more coherent and told me she actually lived a few miles away but got lost for a bit. I put her in my car and drove her to a mobile home a few miles away. She went inside, so I was assuming she really lived there or I prayed she did. I left there bawling as I thanked the Lord for interrupting my busyness to help someone in need.

A few days later, I was at the bank and a lady approached me. She said, "I know you are Christi Johnston. My daughter-in-law was the woman you took home the other night. She told me about you stopping to help her. We had been looking everywhere for her and the Lord used you to find her. Thank you for your compassion. She seems to be better this week." I replied, "You are welcome. I just said yes to the Lord and He used my yes to bring her home." The power of our YES changes lives.

The next story I want to share happened as I am writing this chapter. My daughter and I had gone to town for a lunch date. We were sitting still at a stop light when suddenly I felt the jolt of our vehicle being hit. You got it, rear-ended and our necks felt the whiplash. We were okay so I got out to walk to the car behind me.

It was an elderly couple and the lady behind them knocked them into us. The lady was so frail and shaking. Of course, I did not know her but she felt the love of Jesus in me. Immediately I grabbed her hand and told her she was going to be just fine. She complained that her chest hurt because the seat belt tightened across her during impact. I sat there on the side of her car, holding her sweet hand.

She looked at me with tears in her eyes, saying, "Please don't leave me. You make me feel better." I could cry as I write this because I can see her tears and the utter fear in her heart. I told her I wouldn't leave her until help arrived. I did my best to bring her love and comfort.

Once the police arrived, he asked me to move my vehicle over into a parking lot to clear the main path. I did as he asked then stayed in my own vehicle. Around ten minutes later, the police officer knocked on my window and asked if I knew that lady personally. I told him no, I was just trying to calm her. He then replied, "She's calling for you saying, 'I need that pretty blonde lady to come back to me. I need her.'"

I got out of the vehicle and went to her. She said this, "Can you hold my hand again? I just feel better with you here." I know it wasn't me but the Jesus in me that comforted her for He is the Great Comforter.

After everything was over she hugged me and thanked me for being an angel for her. She even kissed my forehead. Uhhh, I am crying as I write this. Weeks went by then one day I checked my mail. She sent me a card and it read, "Thank you for making me feel better the day of the accident. You are a sweet lady that took time for me. You are an angel."

I shared these two personal stories to encourage you to be a Yes person to the Lord, When you say "yes, Lord, yes", He will use you in great capacities to love and serve the Kingdom.

Are you willing and available? I pray your answer is YES.

# Chapter 5
## REST IS A WEAPON

Did you know that rest is a weapon? I had never heard that myself until this last year. I knew we were supposed to rest and keep the Sabbath holy, but the details of "resting in the Lord" came into clarity for me several months ago. You see, rest is not spiritual laziness or weakness; it is a weapon.

There's not much the enemy hates more than someone who refuses to constantly battle fear, worry, and anxiety but instead confidently and intentionally rests in the promises and faithfulness of God. Let's think about this for a moment. How can we ever reflect the light if we are always worn out, downtrodden, and depressed? We can't.

I look at rest now as the number one ingredient in my ability to be used by the Lord. If anyone knows about being worn out and exhausted by life, I do. I have lived most of the past twenty years in Arkansas Children's Hospital with my special-needs daughter. It's a tired that mere sleep can't fix for it is both physical and spiritual.

Many trials we face, we endure them, and then they are over, but my daughter and her disabilities are lifelong. It's not going away until Jesus heals her or we make heaven our home. This is why it is so crucial to allow joy and sorrow to coexist. Just because we have problems doesn't mean we can't be happy.

I openly share our lives because I choose to. Our trials allow us to train for battle. We build our spiritual arsenal by praying in the Holy Ghost, reading the Word, and encouraging ourselves in hymns and songs. If you read David's prayers in the book of Psalms, he lays his heart wide open and calls upon the Lord in his despair and distress. That is exactly what we are to do, for in our weakness He shows Himself strong.

It is vitally important to know when to engage your enemy, but also to know when to rest. Not every battle is our assignment, so we must learn when to put the sword away, lean unto Him, and fight with the weapon of rest.

This past season has been a huge transition for me. About a year-and-a-half ago, I was praying for someone at the altar at church. I wasn't praying for myself or anything to do with me at that moment. When I turned around to step back onto the stage, the Lord spoke a word to me. It literally came so fast that I had to grab my phone and type it out so I wouldn't forget it. This is what He spoke to me on December 13, 2020:

> "Christi, you are entering a season of rest. You will rest in My anointing. Everything in your life will be in rest.

Your work, family, church, finances, marriage, all of it. You will not have to struggle in these areas for you are resting secure in Me. You have put your hand to the plow for well over twenty years faithfully. You are going to rest in My harvest, for where there is rest there is no distress."

The anointing is for the work, the glory is for the rest. What a download He gave me in a matter of minutes. When I am rested, I am so much more powerful in the anointing. I have clarity of mind, therefore it flows more freely from within.

I believe in this season of life the Lord is calling us to align and be vigilant in all that we do. We must protect our anointing at all cost. The darker the world becomes, the brighter we as children of the Light must shine.

"Come to me, all of you who are weary and burdened, and I will give you rest" (Matthew 11:28). Resting in the Lord means we completely trust His provision. We don't have to try to figure it out or help Him out. I can assure you, He doesn't need us to tell Him a better idea. His ways are perfect and His thoughts are higher than ours. We see to the corner but He sees around it.

Through our journey with our medically complex child, the Lord has taught me how to rest in Him. At first, I did not understand the extent of that and all it entailed. As my personal relationship has matured, my knowledge has increased in trusting Him in all things.

Worry is like a rocking chair, it keeps you busy but takes you nowhere. I worried so much in the early years of my daughter's life that I would make myself sick. I stayed nauseated with worry for I did not want to know one more negative diagnosis. That is until Jesus healed me. I want to share about that story now.

My daughter was born with congenital cytomegalovirus. She has half a brain with many disabilities. One day I was sitting on my bedroom floor. Hannah was a few months old at the time and I had just received a phone call from the retina specialist. He told me that she had scar tissue from the virus all on her retinas. Then he said these horrid words, "Your daughter is legally blind." I literally wailed and fell to my knees. The thought of her not being able to see her mommy was devastating! I found myself in a fetal position on my floor.

I turned on the song, "His Strength Is Perfect," sung by Priscilla McGruder. I worshipped my way through the pain. I cried until I didn't have any tears left. I heard the Lord tell me to stand on the Word, so I literally put my Bible on the floor and stood on it.

As I lifted my hands in worship, I felt the pain and depression leave my body. It began at my toes and went up my legs all the way up to my head. I could see a dark cloud lift off of me and make its way through the ceiling. Instantly, I was healed of the depression.

It is a miracle marker in my life. I will never, ever forget the heavenly rest that came upon my soul when this occurred. I laid down for the first time in a year or more with my mind and my spirit rested.

I made an exchange with Jesus that day that forever changed the trajectory of my future. Now, when worry knocks, I send faith to answer it. I could have quit, I could have laid down and allowed depression to take me over, but God!

I have not and will not let the enemy steal my joy. It's not his to have! The joy of the Lord is my strength and my song that gives me the victory all day long. When I lean on Jesus, I can't go wrong. His Word is a lamp unto our feet, the great and only light to our path. It shines in the darkest night and calls all to come and enter in. A city set on a hill cannot be hid.

I love this Scripture, "Return to your rest, my soul, for the LORD has been good to you" (Psalm 116:7, NIV). That is my testimony for sure. He has been so good to me, I cannot tell it all. When you learn the true rest of the Lord, your life will shift just as mine did. It may not happen overnight, but daily strides lead to daily victories. You have to train yourself in self-discipline to speak His promises aloud and not your problems.

**What you focus on, you magnify!**

Do you focus more on your problems or the promises? Whatever you give your time and attention to is what will gain ground in your life. Here are few things I recommend you do to find the rest of the Lord:

- Take time to pray and slow your pace.

- Remove distractions. Sometimes our routines and habits can overwhelm or distract us.

- Bible study. Spending time in God's Word is one way to grow closer to Him.

- Practice thankfulness. Sometimes we focus so much on what we need to do next or our goals that we don't focus on the Lord and we become worn.

- Stillness. Be quiet and give all your attention to His voice. Meditate on His goodness, dwell in His love.

The enemy longs for us to be worn out and unable to rest in the Lord. It's easy for him to get access to us whenever we are weak. This is why it is so important to keep ourselves full of the Word and walk in the Spirit.

When the fiery darts come, and they will, we must be fully dressed in the armor of God. Where the mind goes, the man follows, so we must keep our thoughts in alignment with the Word. Scripture tells us to take captive our thoughts for a reason. If our thoughts are not captive, we walk in the flesh and fulfill its lusts and desires.

I will be honest and tell you that every time I have thought about quitting it was when I was in a lengthy hospital stay and worn out. Rest was a word that wasn't in my vocabulary and led to an emotional breakdown.

You see, when the devil gets you isolated and alone, he uses this sneaky little tool called discouragement to place doubts in your mind. Isn't that what he did with Adam and Eve as well? He made them question, which led to disobeying the Lord.

We must be so careful that we walk in discernment, especially in a season of hardship. When the trial seems like more than you can take, the Pain Taker walks in on the scene. He promises to never leave nor forsake us. It's only when we give a listening ear to the enemy that we question His love for us.

The love of God is greater than anything. His love equips, sustains, encourages, uplifts, and carries us. When we realize how much He truly loves us, we will rest secure in His great and mighty love. In the Word He always reminds us that He will give rest to the weary.

We can try anything this world has to offer, but nothing will give you the love and rest you need besides Jesus. Temporary things are just that, but God's love is from everlasting to everlasting. He is the Author and the Finisher of our faith. On days that I could barely keep my head above water, He would send someone to uplift and encourage me. Never once have I felt alone in a time of need. The body of Christ would surround me with great love.

As born-again believers our life mission should be to love people into the Kingdom. No soul will ever be saved without loving them first.

We have had our fair share of hospital stays that have worn us out for months on end. The love through the body of Christ upheld us not just by prayers but by action. As servants of the Most High, we love and serve others by giving in a time of need. People would send us money, food, personal items, and things to help us during our trial.

I am always so surprised at the people that send us things. It's typically people you don't normally see or even talk to but the Lord places us on their heart. That is the true definition of love. When you meet someone's needs you are the hands and feet of Jesus. It always blesses us to know that people love and genuinely care for our family.

About a year ago, my daughter went into status epilepticus. This is a medical condition that consists of a single seizure or cluster seizures that last longer than five minutes. The brain does not normalize itself in between so you have to put them in a medically induced coma to "reset the brain."

We were in the PICU and I was terrified as I watched my baby girl struggle. She stayed asleep for four days. Talk about scary. The entire time I sat and watched her, I prayed. I prayed for supernatural rest, healing, and peace.

My momma heart was shattered, but I had an encounter with the Lord late one night. I had made my way down to the hospital chapel and buried myself under the pew. I laid upon my Word and reminded the Lord of His promises to me. As I made my way to the front of the chapel, I heard the Lord telling me, "This is not how your story ends."

I knew in that moment the Lord would bring Hannah through once again. We have had so many close calls, but this time I heard Him clearly. He did not bring us this far for our story to end like that. I wrote it out on a piece of paper, thanked Him for the word, and headed back up to the PICU.

I walked around her room as she rested peacefully in a medicated coma. I felt His presence, His power, His love, and His strength lift me. I held that promise in my hand and declared aloud, "This is not how my story will end." On the fifth day, which seemed like 300, my baby girl opened her beautiful eyes. As soon as she heard my voice, she gave me a little grin. What peace filled my heart to know she was still with me and His promise held true once again.

I have had hundreds of encounters with the Lord. I have experienced too much for anyone to tell me He is not real or He can't. No one, and I mean no one, can take my experiences away from me. You simply can't argue with an experience.

Our trial with Hannah has brought so many people hope. Doctors, nurses, therapists, you name it, have seen the hand of

God resting upon our life. She is a true miracle that reflects the light of Jesus every single day. The Kingdom lives inside of us. We have the ability to shift atmospheres because the King walked into the room.

I believe the PICU at Arkansas Children's Hospital recognizes King Jesus. Every encounter I have had, He met me there with a word, wisdom, and discernment. My soul has entered rest after my encounters and my sleep was sweet. I'm not saying everything always turned out like I wanted, but what I can tell you is He has kept her. He has been faithful to me and mine.

Every day that I have Hannah is another day for a miracle. Her radiant light is angelic. She is as close to a sinless soul as anyone can be. Through her disabilities I have learned the meaning of selfless love and how to place the needs of others before my own. I am a better person because of these hardships. I have learned how to press in and press on. I have learned that I am stronger than I think I am and know I can do all things through Christ who strengthens me. Not just some things but ALL.

I read a book called *Sacred Rest* by Saundra Dalton-Smith. It really opened my eyes up to the various types of rest that we actually need. There are seven types of rest she covers in this book: physical, mental, spiritual, emotional, sensory, social, and creative. She explains how a deficiency in any of these areas can affect our overall health and rest.

Balance is key in life. Staying busy is easy but resting is more of a challenge. This book helped me personally figure out what area I needed more rest in. I encourage you to read it while you rest.

It is a good thing to lie back in your recliner and rest in the Lord. You aren't lazy or weak. You are sharpening your sword for the battle ahead. I believe the enemy has convinced us to stay busy so we will never enter into the rest of God. He absolutely knows that we are powerful when we are well rested so he tries to stop us by distractions and busyness.

In Luke chapter 10:38-42 is the story of Mary and Martha. Martha is working really hard to welcome Jesus into her home so she is busy, busy, busy. Her sister Mary on the other hand decides to sit at the feet of Jesus and rest. They both had a choice to make that day. One was distracted by the busyness of work while the other recognized the importance of sitting at the feet of the Lord.

Martha asked Jesus, "Do You not care that my sister has left me to do all the work by myself? Tell her to help me." But the Lord answered, "Martha, Martha, you are worried and distracted by many things; there is need of only thing, Mary has chosen the better part, which will not be taken away from her." We can clearly see how priorities are key in our lives. If it is important to us, we make a way. If it isn't we make an excuse for our busyness.

***I don't want to be busy, I want to be fruitful.*** Give yourself the opportunity to lean unto Jesus. Sit at His feet and rest. You will be surprised what you learn when you simply get quiet and listen.

# Chapter 6
## SHINE BRIGHT

The first thing I do in the mornings when I wake up is let the sunshine in. I walk through my house and open every curtain and blind. My oldest daughter thinks that is the strangest thing because she keeps hers closed most of the time.

I live in the country with no other houses around so I don't have onlookers. Meg lives in town so she says she doesn't want others peeking in. I do understand that, but I cannot stand for my home to be dark. I have lamps on all the time with light shining bright. When I begin my day, the light helps me to get awake and alerts my mind and body that it's daytime.

In Genesis 1:2-5 it reads, "Now the earth was formless and empty, darkness covered the surface of the watery depths, and the spirit of God was hovering over the surface of the waters. Then God said 'Let there be light,' and there was light. God saw that the light was good, and God separated the light from the darkness. God called the light 'day' and the darkness he called 'night.' There was an evening, and there was a morning: one day" (CSB).

***The voice of our King is mighty. One word and boom: it all began.***

"In the beginning was the Word, and the Word was with God, and the Word was God. He was with God in the beginning. All things were created through Him, and apart from Him not one thing was created. In Him was life, and that life was the light of men. That light shines in the darkness, and yet the darkness did not overcome it" (John 1:1-5, CSB).

As a child of God, we are children of light. God's illuminating light shines in and through us. We carry the light of the world inside of us for we are "carriers of the glory." How amazing is it that the King of Kings and Lord of Lords abides in our heart? He loves us enough to make a deposit into our spirit with His Holy Spirit.

When Jesus was with His disciples, He told them, I must go away but I will not leave you comfortless. I will send back the Comforter, the Holy Ghost, whom the Father will send in My name. He will teach you all things.

The Holy Ghost is your best friend. He will lead, guide, help, discern, comfort, and convict. Without the Holy Ghost, you are a soul that wanders around and doesn't know what direction to go. He is our internal GPS system that navigates our life to keep us on track. Unlike Siri, the Good Book never gets us lost. His Spirit might reroute us but it's for our own good. His Word is the road map that keeps His children shining bright for the world to see.

You are a carrier of more things than you could possibly know. A carrier of love, light, goodness, mercy, gentleness, patience, self-control—did I hit a nerve with anyone there? If any of these are areas you struggle with, focus on every Scripture that will help you improve in that area. People watch to see if we are walking the walk or just talking the talk. May we never be found to be a hypocrite that says we are of the light but carrying around darkness. We are a separated people called unto righteousness and holiness.

If the world runs to it, we should run the opposite way. We were born to stand out—not to fit in. That's an area that is hard for many to accept, but it's by His Spirit that we are protected from the darkness of the world.

Light and dark are polar opposites, just like cold and hot. We have to choose one or the other. In Revelation 3:16 it says, "So, because you are lukewarm—neither hot nor cold—I am about to spit you out of my mouth" (NIV). Sounds like to me, the choice is to stay hot!

If our passion wanes, we become stagnant and complacent, which eventually leads to half-heartedness. When we surrender our hearts to Christ, we are pliable clay in His hands. Willingly, we lay down things that cause our flesh to stumble or to sin. We cultivate that by praying, reading the Word, and fasting. If we fail to feed our spirit, our flesh rises above our spirit. This is never a good thing and surely dulls our light from shining brightly.

Your steadiness in your walk with Jesus is so important. People don't want to follow someone that is in/out, up/down, light/dark. No, they follow children of the light that are steady and consistent. Even in trials, even when they don't get their way, they still serve Jesus. Through the valley and on the mountaintop they do not wane in their faith.

People who shine from within never need a spotlight, for they shine daily just by what they carry. Some people never talk to you or need you until they are in a crisis of faith. Be thankful you are the light that comes to their mind when they are in the darkness.

Have you ever been with someone and you think, *I feel a good spirit from them*, or rather, *I feel a bad spirit?* That is called discernment and you operate in that by the Holy Ghost. Romans 8:16-17 says, "The Spirit Himself bears witness with our spirit that we are children of God, and if children, then heirs—heirs of God and joint heirs with Christ, if indeed we suffer with Him, that we may also be glorified together" (NKJV).

I always feel like it's a magnetic pull when two believers cross paths. Their spirits almost reach out and greet one another for they recognize the family of God. Likewise when we pass someone that carries a dark spirit, the hairs on our neck stand up. It is an intuition from the Holy Ghost that lets us know they are of a different family. It's then that our hearts should radiate the love of Jesus and throw a lifeline out for them to be saved. My pastor taught a series once on "Holy Ghost Intersections." It was about the Lord allowing certain people to cross paths at a pivotal moment in time.

My oldest daughter was in TJ Maxx and a lady approached her and asked if she was my daughter. She replied yes. The lady then proceeded to tell her that she used to go to church with me and I also did her hair. Next, she poured her heart out to Meg and told her she was suicidal and at the lowest of low. This is a divine Holy Ghost intersection. The Lord placed Meg there for this lady. Meg asked if she could hug and pray for her. The lady then wept on her shoulder as she ministered to her.

A few days later I received a text from this lady who told me she knew God had placed my daughter there just for her. She told me after they hugged and prayed she felt so peaceful and calm. Isn't that just like our Jesus to place His children right where He needs them to be? He loves us so much that He will have someone waiting for us when there is a need. I believe that.

One area I really want to focus on in this chapter is how YOU can shine bright every single place that you are. "No one after lighting a lamp puts it under the bushel basket, but on the lampstand, and gives light to all in the house. In the same way let your light shine before others, so that they may see your good works and give glory to your Father in heaven" (Matthew 5:15-16, CSB).

When you carry His light inside of you, the whole world should see it. Others will be drawn to you and might not even know why. That's when you have the opportunity to share what you carry. It's Jesus living on the inside that makes the difference in you.

I know there have been times in your life when you have been around someone and you always feel better after you leave their presence. You leave uplifted, encouraged, and blessed. That's because you can tell they have been saturated in the presence of the Lord. The aroma they carry has a beautiful fragrance that draws others to it.

I read this story online somewhere and it really moved my heart so I want to share it with you. Your life carries the aroma of where you've been and what you've done. When I was a child there were times I would go down to the garbage dump and dig around the garbage to see what I could find that others threw away. It was fun!

Sometimes I would bring home a broken toy or rejected artifact that someone else found worthless. The problem was after I dug around in the garbage, when I rode my bike back home, the smell of other people's garbage came back with me. You could tell where I had been.

I love the fact that in the early days of the first-century church they took notice that the followers of Christ had been with Jesus. Let's protect the aroma of our lives. You will always find what you look for, whether that is Dirty Garbage or Destined Glory. We belong to the Tribe of Christ, whose sweet aroma of love replaces garbage with grace. Protect the aroma of your faith. Love is a sweet-smelling aroma.

There are many ways that we prepare ourselves to carry such a sweet aroma around. Here are a few things to help you carry efficiently.

- Bathe yourself in the Word and prayer. This means to be spiritually consumed in the glory so your aroma is that of love.
- Protect your anointing. What you carry is priceless. Don't allow anything to contaminate your precious oil.
- Put on every piece of the armor of God daily. Do not leave your house half-dressed. The fiery darts will come as soon as you step out into this dark world.
- Walk in the Spirit. Discerning of spirits is an absolute must. You must be able to tell the truth from a lie.
- Keep your thoughts captive and bring them under the subjection of Christ.
- Repent quickly if you find yourself walking in the flesh.

There isn't anything the enemy hates more than a bright light that shines for Christ. The closer you walk with Jesus, the more he hates you. He will try everything he can to make you back up, trip up, or shut up. But I have great news to tell you! Jesus gave us, the believer, all power and authority over the enemy.

He can only tempt us. It's ultimately our decision, through our free will, to choose to quit. Don't ever take the bait. Keep pressing in and on for Jesus. Run your race to win it, and finish, hearing Jesus say, "Well done." If others follow you, make sure you are following Christ.

> "And do not be conformed to this world, but be transformed by the renewing of your mind, that you may prove what is that good and acceptable perfect will of God" (Romans 12:2, NKJV).

There should be a significant difference in the life of the believer. We should not walk, talk, or act like the world. When our minds are transformed our desires shift. Things we once loved we now hate and things we once hated we love. That is what the love of Christ does. He makes all things new, bright, and shiny.

Recently I had a few light bulbs go out in my bathroom. I didn't realize when I replaced them that I had LED white lights. Whoa…the light was so much brighter it nearly blinded me. I could see things even on my face that I couldn't see before with the regular light bulbs.

Oh my, the white hair was shining bright on my head too. Whew, in fact the light was so much brighter after I changed out the bulbs, I could only use two bulbs instead of four. My husband flipped the light on and told me the lights were blinding. We can think of this spiritually as well.

### *Has your light grown dim?*

Did you once shine bright but suddenly you seem a bit dull? Maybe you have a small light but it's not as bright anymore. Try cleaning your lamp. Maybe there is unforgiveness, bitterness, offense, or unresolved issues that may be the cause of your dullness.

Clean your lamp through prayer, repentance, and renewal. All you have to do is draw close to Him and He will shine His light in the places that need to be cleaned up. It is never fun to get a Holy Ghost spanking, but He chastises those He loves. It helps us to grow, mature, and be of excellent character.

Daily I pray this prayer:

Lord Jesus, search me and know me. Create in me a clean heart and a right spirit. If I have done anything to sin against You, please forgive me. I want to pursue Your heart in all I do. Help me to line myself up with Your Word. I want to be Your hands and feet to win souls for Your Kingdom. Place people in my path today that I can share Your love and goodness with.

In Jesus' name. Amen.

Our hearts must be tender to His love. Love is what will win people to the Kingdom. We will be known by our love and generosity. One thing I have noticed in the Scripture is the compassion Jesus had. Not one time did He ever perform a miracle until compassion was flowing. If we aren't compassionate, our light will never shine bright. Unfortunately we live in a world consumed with self. What's in it for me? How can it help me? What about me?

It's truly sad but it's where we are. We should never be so consumed with ourselves that our compassion for others wanes. My nineteen-year-old special-needs daughter has made me who I am. She has taught me selfless love, compassion, patience, and goodness. I am better because of my trials.

It has been a training ground for character building. I have trained myself to listen for the voice of the Lord so I can have complete clarity in her care. I am not saying I always get it right, but I can tell you, I have built trust with her care team at ACH.

At the time I write this book Hannah is nineteen and nonverbal, I have to be in tune with her and the Lord at all times to know how to care for her every need. Each hospital stay I always, always try to find the silver lining. Whether it be to share our story, give the nurse a compliment, or buy someone else's lunch in the cafeteria, I try to represent our Lord. He loves and cares for every single one of us so much that He bled, died, and rose again for you and for me.

We all lead such different lives but that is what is so amazing about our Lord. He is omniscient, omnipotent, and can be with you while He is with me. Truly an ever-present help and always right on time. Jehovah Jireh, my Provider, He sees, He knows, and He provides for every need we have.

Since I'm on the topic of being all about self, are you a giver or a taker? Yikes, think about that for a minute. In Acts 20:35 Jesus Himself said, "It is more blessed to give than to receive." I can honestly tell you that I am a giver. It makes me so happy to give to others, whether it is a physical, spiritual, or financial need. It fulfills me like nothing else can!

I honestly look for daily opportunities to be a blessing on purpose. I will go out of my way to make sure I serve others first. Not only have I learned that from the Word but by taking care of my daughter. Her needs always come before mine. Every morning I spend about thirty to forty-five minutes crushing medicine, changing her diaper, etc., before I ever tend to anything for myself. This type of serving is not only biblical but absolutely necessary. We love because He first loved us, right?

We love others not just by words but action. Our love walk should be evident by how we serve others. That is how a daily turn reflects the light. We allow the Lord to turn us that day how He wants to use us. It's all about Jesus. When we serve others, we serve Him. Everything that we do should be unto Him. Whether we take care of our children, wash the dishes, clean the house, or cook dinner, it's unto Him.

When I drive to work I like to have my prayer time. Usually I have about twenty-five minutes to pray. I talk to the Lord just like He is sitting in the passenger seat. I ask Him who we are going to minister to today. Is there anything specific I need to look at on my schedule so I can be available for a need? I truly do this. If I put Jesus first and plan my day around Him, I never have to find time to work Him into my schedule. I believe wholeheartedly that Jesus deserves the best of me—not the rest of me. Oh how He loves our firstfruits and not the leftovers.

By trade I am a hairstylist but also an ordained minister of the Gospel. I use my time behind-the-chair to shine bright for Jesus, not only to help others feel beautiful on the outside but the inside as well. If they need prayer, I pray for them right then. If they need a hug, my arms are available; an ear to hear, I listen.

I want my clients to feel better after they have been in my chair. They pay for a service, so my extra love and kindness could be an added blessing to them. I never want someone to dread when they come to sit in my chair but rather be excited to see me.

Things like walking in love, kindness, a smile, a hug, a compliment, that's what this world needs. Sometimes people don't need a Scripture but a warm meal and a hug. Maybe they just need someone to listen to them as they share their struggles. That, my friend, is being like Jesus.

The Lord always opens up a door for us to minister if we look. I can absolutely promise you that people wait on you to be the one that makes a difference for them. Think about when we get to heaven, who will be able to say to you, "Because you cared and shared the Gospel with me, I made it." I pray that is on your heart daily. Those that know me well know that my heart is for people. I cannot imagine not feeling the burden to win souls.

Not a day of my life passes by that I don't thinking about someone to lead closer to the feet of Jesus. We are called to be ministers, maybe not pulpit ministers, but to share the Gospel of Jesus Christ.

**Go ye therefore and make disciples. That is our life mission.**

There is an old song that goes like this:

> *Lord, lay some soul upon my heart,*
> *And love that soul through me;*
> *And may I bravely do my part*
> *To win that soul for Thee.*
> *Some soul for Thee, some soul for Thee,*
> *This is my earnest plea;*
> *Help me each day, on life's highway,*
> *To win some soul for Thee*
> *Lord, lead me to some soul in sin,*
> *And grant that I may be*
> *Endued with power and love to win*
> *That soul, dear Lord, for Thee.*
> *To win that soul for Thee, my Lord,*

*Will be my constant prayer;*
*That when I've won Thy full reward*
*I'll with that dear one share.*[4]

---

4  Baylus Benjamin McKinney (1886-1952), "Lord, Lay Some Soul Upon My Heart," hymnal.net, https://www.hymnal.net/en/hymn/h/932.

# Chapter 7
## BEAUTIFUL PATTERNS

As the Lord spoke to my heart about writing this book, I envisioned beautiful patterns. I could see such bright colors when I would close my eyes, it brought a smile to my face. I designed the book cover how I saw it in prayer. I didn't just see colors but promises that unfolded in my life as seasons shifted. The kaleidoscope got its name from the Greek word "kalos," meaning beautiful, and "skopien," to view. Just knowing that makes me smile, for we all enjoy a beautiful view, right?

Typically it's a breathtaking view from a mountaintop or somewhere as we recognize the beauty of His creation. He has made all things beautiful. In Ecclesiastes chapter 3:1-8 we learn that to everything there is a season and a purpose under heaven. Seasons come and seasons go, but the Lord remains faithful to us through it all. I can most definitely tell you that I have been through every season imaginable.

When I began my walk with the Lord, that was the most joyous season ever. I was newly married, in love with my husband

and Jesus. We set the world ablaze and shared our newfound love in one another and in Christ. But just like a new car, the new wears off. Just like you make strict rules not to eat or drink in that new car, before you know it, there are french fries, crushed-up Cheerios, and soda spilled on the carpet. It becomes a mess as the new has worn off.

That happens in our relationship with Jesus. It is never intentional, but we become lazy and allow our prayer life to slip, our Bible reading isn't a priority, and then we are downtrodden. It's a vicious cycle that steals the joy out of our season.

One thing I have learned is my life can be as beautiful as I want it to be. It's me that messes it up. When I seek other things first and not Jesus, the beauty seems to fade. I want to encourage you as you read this to find your joy in Jesus. Your joy is not found in your circumstances, your spouse, your children, or your friends. Your true joy is and has to always be found in Jesus. The joy of the Lord is your strength and your song.

When life doesn't go as you had planned, when the kids are out of control, when there isn't enough money to pay the bills… God is still good. You can still have joy even if your life is out of control. I know because I have been through it. I had this beautiful, perfect life planned out. You know, the one with the perfect husband, children, and home, it is all perfect. Well, it didn't go as planned. My plans were hindered, therefore I had a choice to be pitiful or powerful.

At first I allowed myself to go to the "pity party" but realized very quickly that was not the life I wanted. I prayed until Jesus allowed me to behold His beauty and see from His point of view. His ways are so much higher than ours. We see to the corner but He sees around it.

I could not understand how all things could be beautiful when my daughter was born missing half of her brain. It wasn't until my perspective shifted that I saw everything that was good and not bad. You see, when Jesus fills our hearts, our vision changes. Instead of focusing on the problems, I set my heart on His promises. That was not easy nor did it happen overnight, but it happened over a twenty-year period of walking by faith and not by sight.

He showed me how Hannah was shaping my family's life as a testimony of His love and grace. Our story was for His glory for the world to see. As we reflected His light, a beautiful testimony of His goodness began to arise.

We have shared our life openly, with our trials, to encourage others to hold on to faith. When everything seems hopeless, He is our hope. When the beautiful season fades into the abyss of darkness, we have a light of great beauty that shines in the darkness to lead us out. The splendor and majesty of our Lord leads us to know Him more and more.

Through times and seasons we can see beautiful patterns of how His hands of mercy have held and kept us. Even in the darkest times, He has never once left us nor forsaken us. I had a choice to make when the hardest trial of my life began. I could run to Jesus or from Him. I am so thankful I ran to Him.

There are no words to explain His faithfulness or His goodness to my family. We have had more trials and hardships than one can imagine, but He never once left us to figure it out. I am so thankful He is not a "love 'em-and leave 'em" God. He is forever faithful and true.

I ask you to see the beauty in your trial. Instead of asking the Lord, "Why do I have to go through this? Why me?" Ask Him, "What can I learn through this? Help me to grow through this and not just go through it."

I read this story somewhere and it is perfect to share in this chapter. There was a man who had four sons. He wanted his sons to learn not to judge things too quickly. So he sent them each on a quest to go and look at a pear tree that was a great distance away.

The first son went in the winter, the second in the spring, the third in the summer, and the youngest son in the fall. When they had all gone and come back, he called them together to describe what they had seen.

The first son said that the tree was ugly, bent, and twisted. The second son said no, it was covered with green buds and full of promise. The third son disagreed. He said it was laden with blossoms that smelled so sweet and looked so beautiful, it was the most graceful thing he had ever seen. The last son disagreed with all of them. He said it was ripe and drooping with fruit, full of life and fulfillment.

The man then explained to his sons that they were all right, because they had each seen but one season of the tree's life. He told them that you cannot judge a tree, or a person, by only one season, and that the essence of who they are and the pleasure, joy, and love that come from that life can only be measured at the end, when all seasons are up.

If you give up when it is winter, you will miss the promise of your spring, the beauty of your summer, and the fulfillment of your fall. Don't judge a life by one difficult season. Don't let the pain of one season destroy the joy of all the rest.

***To everything there is a season.***

When I look back over my life, I can definitely see every season I have gone through. Someone once said that you are typically coming out of a battle or going into one. Life is full of surprises, but our Lord is never surprised, for He orders our steps. I believe that the way we act and react to our battles determines our destiny.

We have all made wrong choices along the way, but it taught us the right lesson. One of my favorite Scriptures is found in Luke

6:45, "For out of the abundance of the heart the mouth speaks." What do we have stored up in our heart? Whatever we have stored up is what will come out in our conversations.

***If we complain, we remain; if we praise, we will be raised.***

Many years ago a friend went through a hard trial. She complained about everything that was wrong, which led her to see nothing right. I tried my best to have her glance at her problems and keep her gaze on the Lord, but she couldn't see the good for the bad. She was blinded by this dark season, therefore the sun could not shine.

As I counseled with her, I heard the Lord tell me that she needed a spiritual heart transplant. She had years upon years of bitterness, offense, and unforgiveness built up in her heart. I encouraged her to pray and release all of this, but she said she didn't feel it. Listen, we can't be moved by our feelings. Our feelings lie to us and lead us astray. Unfortunately, she wasn't willing to let it go, and it did not end well.

I want to encourage you, the reader, to stop and reflect upon the season you are in this moment. You must know the season you are in so you can hear the voice of the Lord in clarity. If you are in a season of "rest" but you are trying to " build," it won't work. If you are trying to do things in your timing and not God's, it won't work. If you have to force it, it is not the season or the time.

When the time is right, the Lord will open the door and you will walk through it with ease. You know how I know? I have done it wrong and I have done it right. I can tell you one thing, God has perfect timing. He is rarely early, never late, but always right on time.

When I am in walking in the right season in the Spirit, it creates beautiful patterns in my life. Things flow easily and the glory of the Lord is tangible. All things are working together for the good. It's as if I can see in the Spirit all the beauty of His splendor. The way seems too easy but it's because I'm following His lead, walking in a "holy ease."

As we grow in our maturity in our walk with Christ we are able to move in and out of the Spirit easily. I can clean my house or change a diaper and within seconds the glory has settled upon me where I am operating in the Spirit.

I don't have to go repent or pray for thirty minutes to get my heart right, for I am continually walking in the Spirit. All I have to do is keep one hand in the earth and one in the heavenlies and pull down the super with my natural. I believe this is an area that believers do not operate in enough. In 2 Timothy 4:2 it tells us to "Preach the word; be prepared in season and out of season" (NIV). That means that we are to be faithful and ready to do whatever we need to do in good or bad circumstances. All throughout the day we should have a praise on our lips and a song in our heart.

I woke up during the night with a song on my heart. I sang it when I got up. The Lord gave that to me in the night and all day long I let it be a beautiful praise to Him as I went through my day. It was this chorus:

> *God's been good to me*
> *God's been good to me.*
> *When I think of what the Lord has done in my life*
> *I know God's been good to me.*

I was able to encourage myself in the Lord as I thanked Him for His goodness to me. In the book of Psalms, David poured his heart out in prayer and praise to the Lord. He called unto Him day and night. In distress and even in despair he continually offered up praise as he called upon the mighty name of Jesus.

No matter where we are in life, Jesus promises He will never leave us nor forsake us. If you aren't as close to God as you once were, who moved? I can promise you it wasn't Him. If you seek Him you will find Him. He is a God that changes not. We may not always understand the whys of the time or the season, but through it all we must trust His master plan. Even when we can't see it, He always works behind the scenes for our good.

If I had my way, my daughter would never have been born disabled. I mean, what parent would ever want their child to be born unhealthy? No one. My point in this is that even though I don't understand it, even though I didn't choose it, it doesn't mean that God doesn't love me less than others. We live in a sinful world where disease and sickness are a real part.

Unfortunately, we are not immune to all this world has to offer. People get sick, things happen, and every person has an appointed time to die. What is wonderful though, this world is not our permanent home. It is a temporary dwelling that we are just passing through.

In heaven there will be no more sickness, pain, or sorrow. We will all be healthy and whole, with glorified bodies. So even though seasons in this life are tough, we will be in the permanence of heaven soon, and that beautiful season will never end. We will live with Jesus for eternity and spend our days crying, "Holy, holy, holy is the Lamb of God." Oh, what a day that will be!

We must occupy until He comes to take us home. The Bridegroom is coming after His beautiful bride and forever we will live and reign with Him! Streets of gold, gates of pearl, mansions, and glorious splendor wait for us. The Word says those who endure to the end will be saved. Whatever season you are in right now, make up your mind that you will not quit but endure until the end.

I am in the second half of my life now. This is a new season for me and I have to adapt to the changes that age brings to me. I am currently 46 years old as I type this chapter. Whew, growing older is not for the faint of heart.

By the way, the Scripture tells us if you faint in the day of adversity, your strength is small. I have a made-up mind that I will not faint but endure until the end. Everything I have been through, I believe, has prepared me for my NOW. I had to go through seasons to grow.

I would never have been offered an associate pastor position with no experience. Writing books, evangelizing, speaking at conferences, and my last eight years as pastor was all training for this newest season.

Building the Kingdom and winning souls never goes out of season. Our approaches may change but the Gospel message never changes. We love because He first loved us! He gave His life so we could live! Look around you and embrace your season. Pray and ask the Lord to reveal to you what season you are in. Then wait on His perfect timing to do what He asks you to do.

As you read the Word, pray, and spend time in His presence, you will have clarity to what He calls you to do. Remember, what He calls you to do is for you. Everyone has different callings and assignments, so walk yours out hand in hand with Jesus. Don't let anyone talk you out of it or lead you astray. Run your race with Jesus and endure until the very end. Stay in your lane; there is no traffic in your own lane. You can go at whatever speed He calls you to.

"But they that wait upon the Lord shall renew their strength; they shall mount up with wings as eagles; they shall run, and not be weary; and they shall walk and not faint" (Isaiah 40:31, KJV).

I am determined that the second half of my life will be the best half of my life. I have grown in wisdom and character in the first half. May it be the most fruitful season yet! Your latter days can be truly greater than the former if your attitude toward life facilitates it. Your perspective on life can open the door to fullness and joy or lack and oppression.

Your attitude is everything. Learn to develop the inner beauty of your heart. Attributes like kindness, love, gentleness, purity, faith, and joy will reflect in your outward appearance. There is nothing more beautiful than a pure, kind, and loving heart. If you are positive within, it will manifest outwardly.

You were not created to have a cursed life. You were created to have an abundant and blessed life. When God created mankind, God blessed them saying, "Be fruitful and multiply" (Genesis 1:22). You were made for a full and overflowing life on earth.

# Chapter 8

## FACES

As I researched the most fascinating parts of a kaleidoscope, one particular area was highlighted to me. It is of the shape of a triangular prism with two triangular faces and three rectangular faces. Each way you turn the prism, faces appear. Just as we are turned each day to reflect His light, we see individual faces of people. I truly believe someone's breakthrough and blessing is dependent on you rising to be who God has called you to be. When they see the hope in your face, they know they can do it too!

Many times as I lie in bed or am in a time of prayer, the Lord will show me someone's face. That typically means I need to pray for the person, or He gives me a word immediately after the vision. Sometimes it's not a face I see, but I will hear a name of an individual as well.

Within the past month, I can tell you of two different faces the Lord has placed before me so vividly. Now let me tell you, I have not been thinking or praying for either of these people when the vision came. I believe wholeheartedly that the Lord places someone on your heart when they are in need of something. Whatever it may be for, it's for divine purpose.

The first individual that came into my mind happened a few weeks ago. I always ask the Lord to lay people on my heart that need prayer. I woke up at 2:30 a.m. and saw this man's face in my mind. I couldn't understand why until I woke up and the Spirit spoke to me about him. You see, this man used to think the world of me and mine. When he served Jesus, we were part of his family. But as soon as he backslid, he wanted no part of us.

I'm sure you have noticed that darkness doesn't like a bright, shining light. It cringes at the thought of it. I saw his face in my prayer and instantly I realized I hadn't seen any of his Facebook posts for a while. As soon as I thought that, the Holy Ghost said, "Of course you haven't. He deleted you. Your light was too bright!" I scrolled to look him up and it said "Add friend" button, which means you are a friend no more. You have been deleted!

Have any of you been deleted in real life, like dropped, blocked, or canceled? I have more times than I care to share, but I can promise you, it was not because I was mean or ugly. People don't like truth. When they feel like you judge them or you have a difference of opinion, they typically turn the other way. Not just on social media but in life.

The Lord made us all special in every way. There are no two people in this world exactly alike. Down to our fingerprints, it is individualized. This makes the world go around because we all look different and like different things. Life would be totally boring if we all looked, liked, and acted exactly the same. Just because we all like different things doesn't make one right and one wrong. It's okay for everyone to be different.

I can testify to the fact that people are just people. I can see something one way, you can see it another, but the key is to give grace and mercy. Just because I love red and you don't, doesn't mean we can't be friends.

A lady told me that her best friend told her that if they didn't go to the same church, they couldn't be friends any longer. Weird, right? She was like, "Um, I didn't know we were part of a cult." Some things just make no sense, but like I said, we are all different in our opinions.

Opinions are like noses. We all have one! Don't offer your opinion unless it is asked for. I learned that the hard way. Our lives are made up of chapters and seasons. Just because we have a bad chapter doesn't mean it's a bad life. There are people that we think will be part of our story for life but they were just meant for a chapter.

It's sad when you want them to be a lifer, but God says no, only a chapter. That's why we have to hang on to people, places, and things loosely. It's all temporal, and if we aren't careful, we look for those things to fulfill us. Only Jesus can do that. He is the only one that can fill the hole in our heart. Our heart is His home and we are to abide with Him.

The next face the Lord flashed before me happened as I was holding Hannah and reading a book. Out of nowhere and I mean nowhere, this lady's face flashed before me. Instantly I heard the Lord say, "Message her with these words, 'I know all and I see all; truth prevails.' " I had absolutely no idea why I saw her face and was given that word for her, but I obeyed the Spirit as He instructed.

She messaged me right back with this, "You have no idea! I am going through one of the roughest battles of my life right now and need every prayer warrior I can to stand in the gap for my family. I needed this word!" You never know when, where, what, or how the Lord will use you.

Faces, faces, and more faces I see daily in my quiet time. It is souls I see, but the faces that flash before me have a soul that will spend eternity in heaven or in hell. It is our duty as born-again believers to allow the Lord to turn us each day for Kingdom use. However He wants to use us, we must be willing to obey. That's all He wants is our obedience.

"The fruit of the righteous is a tree of life, and he that winneth souls is wise" (Proverbs 11:30, KJV).

I want to be found wise and win souls daily for the Kingdom. I pray that millions would say, "Because of YOU, I have made it to heaven." Let that be our prayer as we see faces of those that need Jesus. Your life not only reflects the light, but your face, words, demeanor, and attitude draw people in or push them away.

Loving God and loving people is a life mission that we all must say YES to. You don't have to agree with someone to love them, but you have to love them no matter what. "Let all that you do be done in love" (1 Corinthians 16:14, ESV).

The Lord has called me to be a spiritual mother. I want to share the story behind this. The past eight years that I was the associate pastor the Lord used me to hold women as a mother would her child. My arms are called to comfort the broken, hold the needy, and encourage the weak. He has given me this gift and developed it in me through my special-needs child, Hannah, who is nonverbal.

I have had to diligently seek His voice for guidance, clarity, and provision in my care for her. Since she can't communicate with me, I rely on the Lord fully to be my true Helper. Because of this my sense of knowing in the Spirit has been enhanced, therefore I know and I see things about people. I have been given spiritual gifts to know the words to say as I hold these women in my arms and comfort them with my love.

It sounds strange to those that aren't around me, but it is truly a heaven-sent gift He has given me. My senior pastor calls me "Momma Jesus" as my nickname because when we see a need in a female, he says they need their Momma Jesus to hold them.

I believe hugs heal. You can speak to someone, pray with them, and even encourage them, but the touch of a caring heart and hug bring peace to the soul. Jesus is the Peace Speaker who calms hearts while He uses our hands and arms to embrace others.

As we walk in obedience to the Lord, He directs our steps. He brings people into our life, our workplaces, our churches etc., so we can help them grow in their walk with Christ. So many give their heart to Jesus and are never discipled. This is why people don't stay in church or in a personal relationship with the Lord. It is our job as spiritual mothers and/or fathers to teach them. The Great Commission in Matthew 28:16-20 tells us that Jesus calls on His followers to go make disciples.

That is our calling as a follower of Jesus. If we are going to heaven, we need to take everyone that we can with us. This isn't a solo ride where we go at it alone, but this is a nationwide journey for all to go.

Jesus tells us in Matthew 24:14 that "this Gospel of the Kingdom will be preached in the whole world as a testimony to all nations and then the end will come." (NIV) We have work to do and time is short. The harvest is plentiful but the laborers are few. Are you willing to unbusy yourself to go hold the broken and disciple them?

I know for me that I can't rest when I see faces before me that are lost. Oh, my soul is grieved knowing that they might not know Jesus. We have to work while it is yet day. Remember, the worth of souls is great in the sight of God. The angels in heaven rejoice over one sinner that repents.

They have a Holy Ghost party celebrating your name being written in the Lamb's Book of Life. I have had women sit in my salon chair that wept and gave their lives to Jesus right then and there. I have sat on my salon floor and held the broken after a hair service and led them straight to Jesus' feet. I cannot tell you how many hundreds, yes, hundreds of times that I sat with the broken, and wiped their nose and tears.

That is agape love and the love Jesus wants us to walk in. You see, people are attracted to you because of what you carry. If you carry the light of Jesus Christ, you are a lighthouse that leads broken vessels to the shores of victory.

You don't have to know all the Scriptures, pray a special prayer, or do anything spectacular to win a soul. You share your testimony with them, live and walk it out, and then you disciple them. As you follow Christ, they follow you. It's all about leading people to the cross. If you will just say yes to Jesus and allow Him to fill your mouth, He will do it.

Remember when the Lord called Moses to go before Pharaoh? (Exodus 4) He gave the Lord every excuse he could of why he shouldn't be the one to go speak to Pharaoh. He told the Lord, "You know I am not a man of eloquent speech, I am slow of tongue. I can't do it." The Lord replied, "Who gave man his mouth and who makes them deaf or mute? Is it not I the Lord? Now go, and I will be with your mouth and will teach you what you shall say." He was saying, "You can do this Moses. I will be with you."

Moses kept on until the anger of the Lord kindled and burned upon him. The Lord then proceeded to tell him that He knew his brother Aaron, the Levite, spoke fluently that he would send him to act as a mouthpiece for Moses.

Isn't that how we do the Lord? He calls us to do something and we give Him every excuse of why we are not capable of doing what He has asked us to do. That's when He looks for someone else to use. If we want to have excuse abuse, then we will never be used for Kingdom assignments. I know the Lord has to get tired of our excuses.

**Truth is, if we want to do something, we make a way. If not, we make an excuse.**

When Jesus returns to get us, we have to be ready. We are will stand face-to-face with our Lord and Savior. I pray He doesn't have to say, "Depart from Me, you worker of iniquity, I never knew you." Daily we should strive to grow one step closer to our King.

When we seek His face and not His hand, our personal relationship increases. We go to a new level in our journey and experience new things in the spirit realm. To not seek means to not grow. The Holy Ghost teaches us all things as we seek more and more of His presence.

Do you see someone's face in your mind as you read this? I do. Even as I type, I can see faces that need an encounter with Jesus. A true encounter face-to-face that forever changes their destiny.

Back in March of 2023, the Lord spoke to me about hosting "Encounter" services. He told me to build it and they would come. I listened to divine instructions as He gave it to me and built an army of intercessors and worshippers. We did very little advertising, but I can tell you one thing, I heard from the Lord.

Those two services were so packed out that people came from all over the state to join in. The atmosphere was supercharged with such a glory cloud that I thought the roof would literally blow off. There were waves of glory and the voices of the people would sound as a roar across the sanctuary. I can see the faces of the people now.

Wow, just wow! Souls were saved, water baptisms, infillings of the Holy Ghost, and rededications. They were life-changing services all because the Lord instructed me, I obeyed, and many, many people were forever changed because of their personal encounters.

Truly that is what is needed for each of us. When we encounter Jesus personally, we are never the same. Your experience with the Lord is YOURS. It is yours to tell and share to the world. We are made overcomers by the Word of our testimony and by the blood of the Lamb.

When you see a face, see their soul. Don't just pass people by and not care. Glance at their face but pray for their soul. We should be moved with compassion when we see a face before us. Nothing, and I mean nothing else matters in this world if our family and our friends are lost. Heaven is real, hell is real, and your choice is real.

Make sure you have made your reservation in heaven. When He calls you home, may He glance at the Book, see your name, and the millions you brought with you. Jesus sees your face as precious. He thinks of you, He loves you, and He longs to see you face-to-face forever in heaven.

In closing of this chapter, I share a personal story. When I tell you it is personal, it means EVERYTHING to me. About a month ago, I was outside in our hot tub. I go out there late at night a lot to relax and spend time with the Lord. I was having prayer time and it was very cold and dark outside. It was obviously hot in the water but my upper body was up above the water.

All of a sudden, I heard the Lord speak to me about being a spiritual mother. I saw myself as a midwife, per se, but it was spiritual. I was helping women birth things in the Spirit. I wept and my tears were so heavy and hard that they were hitting the water.

I then looked up as a cool breeze blew across me and the Lord gave me an open vision. He called me by name, "Christi, I have called you to be a spiritual mother. You are to help women birth spiritual things. Look up!" I then looked up and saw millions, not just a few women, but armies of women. One by one, I could see their faces. Each one that passed me said this "Christi, thank you! Because you obeyed we made it to heaven. We are here!"

I could not believe my eyes as I watched them pass by me. Some would hug me, some would touch my shoulder, some would stop and cry, but I was frozen in the water as I watched them enter into the gates of heaven. After I came out of the vision, I lay in the water, wept, and praised Jesus for showing me what has and is to come.

I know the spiritual mothers are rising up in this hour! The Deborahs are rising up. The Esthers are shifting atmospheres. The Ruths are taking back what the devil stole from them. The Hannahs are birthing miracles!

# Chapter 9

## MOMENTS, MEMORIES, AND MANDATES

Through life we all have so many special moments and memories we have made with the Lord. This is why I love to journal, for I remind myself of all the things He has done for me. If I have a down day, I can simply open up my journal and remind myself of all the wonderful works of the Lord. I just opened up a random journal entry as I write this and it makes me smile. It states, "Look what the Lord has done! Once again a miracle that I have been seeking Him for, He answered."

If you don't journal I want to encourage you to start today. I have over fifty journals, in all shapes, colors, and sizes of documentation of the good, the bad, and the ugly of my life. I started journaling in 2011, so I have well over thirteen years' worth of my life recorded. I wish I would have started well before then, but unfortunately I didn't. At least I have those years recorded and from here forward.

Moments are fleeting but memories are made for a lifetime. I have so many of them all. As I look back on my life and see everything I have overcome, I stand amazed. Of course, I don't have everything documented, but my memory serves me well on most things.

Some of the most impactful moments and memories I have had are like a marker in my journey. I want to share a few of those to encourage you to never say never. If you tell the Lord you would never do something, He will have you "nevering" like never before!

In 2010 on a random Thursday night, I was spending time with the Lord. I heard Him tell me to start a home Bible study for ladies. I never second-guessed that, and four days later on that Monday night I hosted my first-ever ladies Bible study.

I made a post on social media, shared my heart, and thought, *If I have one lady show up, I will be happy.* I wasn't concerned about a number; I just wanted to be obedient to the Lord. The very first night of the study I had fifteen ladies walk in the door of my home. Some I knew, some I did not know, but what I can tell you is they came hungry for the Lord.

From that first study until 2013 we met together on Monday nights to pray, study the Word, and encourage one another. I would prepare a message, teach it, then we would have prayer meeting. It wasn't an ordinary prayer meeting. We interceded for the lost; people were delivered, healed, and filled with the Holy

Ghost. It was an unbelievable time in the Lord and women came in the droves. I am absolutely not exaggerating when I say weekly we had many new guests.

During our times of prayer, ladies shouted, danced, spoke in tongues, and prophesied over one another. One night a few ladies shouted off my front porch into the field, ran and danced, and prayed in tongues. The Holy Ghost and fire was alive and well here at my address. We then did baptisms. I have videos of me as I baptized ladies in my jacuzzi. They would come up and speak in tongues, free and delivered. It was just, WOW!

One particular moment and memory I want to share is profound. My friend Susan lived under severe anxiety, depression, and suicidal thoughts. She loved the Lord, was saved, and Holy Ghost filled, but the demonic attachments tried to drown her. We all got around her and prayed in the name of Jesus and commanded those evil spirits to flee from her.

She saw a therapist, took a gallon Ziploc bag of pills, and had even planned out how she would take her life. When the name of Jesus was spoken over her in a room full of like-minded believers we watched Susan be instantaneously delivered. Her countenance was different, she had joy, and the gallon Ziploc bag of pills she had with her, never again did she have to take another pill.

There is absolutely no way you can cold-turkey stop that much medication and have zero negative side effects. But when the

Healer stepped in the room for Susan's freedom, the Great Physician took it all. Every bit of it—GONE! I have videos and pictures of it all. An absolute MIRACLE in epic proportion!

Our group kept growing. Of course after Susan's miracle, other ladies came and sought deliverance for the same thing. Soon we outgrew my home. I couldn't fit one more lady in a chair. We were packed to the brim.

It's then the Lord told me, "Make room." I thought, *Lord, I have made all the room that I can.* He then proceeded to tell me to sell my dining room furniture and fill it full of chairs. I thought, *Well, okay!* I had a very nice table hutch full of the beautiful china from my wedding day. I loved it and loved the way it all looked, but I loved Jesus more.

I asked a few ladies in the group if anyone wanted to buy it because it was just too nice and expensive to give away. Besides that, I needed the money to go purchase folding chairs to fill up for souls. Lo and behold, sweet Susan needed it, and not only did her miracle happen in my home, but she also got the dining room of her dreams to place in her home! It was a double blessing for me and for her. I will never, ever forget the moment of her deliverance. God is faithful!

The dining room furniture leaves and about thirty folding chairs were placed in my dining room. I have a large living and dining area so we rearranged it for full capacity. Every single chair was filled within the next two weeks. The pictures and the videos I have and can share are priceless. Memories made for lifetimes made right here in my home.

We were growing so rapidly, my friend Carla and I decided we needed to rent a building to hold everyone. It was a big commitment for it would cost us $100 a week, but we knew the Lord would provide and He always did. Every single week, the rent was paid for by someone.

It outgrew my solo abilities with a special-needs daughter, so my friend, Carla, joined me and we took turns teaching the studies. I can tell you that it was the talk of the town, for real. I even had a pastor of another church stop me in the local grocery store and wanted to know what I was doing down there with his church ladies.

I thought, *What? I'm not doing anything, but the Holy Ghost shows up, shows out, and fills your Baptist ladies with the Holy Ghost and fire.* He was none too happy about it, to be honest. It was clear he carried a spirit of jealousy. All glory to Jesus, the One whom blessings flow.

By the end of 2013, we had named the group Cornerstone Ladies Bible Study and had grown to over seventy-five women. We built an army from my living room to the Matthews Civic Center. We built disciples and helped fulfill the Great Commission. Those precious moments and memories will forever be etched into my heart. I heard the Lord speak, I obeyed, and He took the little I had and turned it into something great.

If you could hear the testimonies from the ladies that were a part of this group, you would be amazed. Maybe one day I will have a reunion to remember the days of small beginnings. But it was honestly never small, for the Holy Ghost moved at will from the very first meeting.

"Do not despise these small beginnings for the Lord rejoices to see the work begin" (Zechariah 4:10, NLT).

Once the Lord shifted my assignment, I evangelized at various churches. I shared our story of our journey with our special-needs daughter, built faith, and encouraged others to keep the faith. Next, that turned into speaking at ladies conferences and holding revivals.

I honestly had no idea what I was doing, but I can tell you the Holy Ghost did. I sought Him, He filled my mouth, and we worked together as a team. From 2013 to 2015 I spoke in over 65 churches. The Lord gloriously saved, filled, and healed hundreds. He used my YES to draw people to Him.

The key to soul winning is to allow the Lord to use you where you are at. Just as my book title, allow Him to turn you each day to reflect His light. If you do that and walk in obedience, you will be a soul winner and a Kingdom builder.

Self has to be moved out of the way. Your focus must be outward and never inward. No matter the cost, a soul is worth it all. If the Lord asks you to do something, use wisdom, but don't allow your flesh to say, "No, I don't want to." I mean, let's be honest, my flesh did not want to sell my beautiful furniture that I loved but my soul said, "Yes, Lord, Yes."

The Scripture plainly tells us that we have to take up our cross daily and follow Him. That means to lay everything else aside and pursue Him at all costs. If we allow the Lord to interrupt our schedules, He will use us more than we could ever imagine. Instead of working Him into your day, work your day around Him.

I know some of you are super schedulers. You have your planner and dates scheduled out to have your snack at 2:00 p.m. I get it, but don't hold so tightly to YOUR schedule. Allow Him to mess it up and move it around, for a soul waits on you to do what He has asked you to do.

If we aren't flexible, the Lord will use someone else. I never want Him to pass me by because my schedule is TOO BUSY for Him. That would be a great tragedy! Ask the Lord what He wants you to do for Him. Listen and obey His directions, for He will guide you in all truth.

> "My sheep hear my voice, and I know them, and they follow Me; and I give them eternal life; and they shall never perish, and no one shall snatch them out of my hand" (John 10:27-28).

He that has an ear let him hear: That means listen up, listen up! He is calling you to do more for His Kingdom. Take a step of faith and trust that He guides your steps all the way.

The Lord gave me mandates two different times in my life. A mandate is an official order or commission to do something. The first mandate He gave me was in 2018. I heard Him as clear as I have ever heard Him. He told me, "Write a second book. Title it, 'I Know Who I Am. Knowing your true identity in Christ.' " He even gave me a clear vision of the cover design, color scheme, and all. I was able to write that book under the anointing of the Holy Ghost in a year. He gave me every single word and helped many come to the knowledge of who they are in Christ.

When the Lord gives you a mandate, you cannot be satisfied until you accomplish it. It is like giving birth to a baby. It grows inside of you and you cannot wait until it is fully developed and brought to life. That is what it felt like to me both times when the mandate was commissioned to me.

I want to share that I had a special place I went to write. It called me by name and said, "Come sit with me a while." I drove to our local lake and sat with my computer at a shaded picnic table and communed with the Lord. He gave me words, wisdom, and knowledge. I always drove away longing to go right back. I think that's how you know it's a mandate. It draws, it pulls, it grows, and satisfies you. The first mandate was complete in 2019.

The second mandate the Lord gave me was in 2022. I always look to mentor someone, help them grow, or simply encourage them. I was invited to go to a ladies retreat in the Smoky Mountains. I wasn't sure when the invite came if I would go because it was a nine-hour drive and I would have to go solo. I prayed about it and didn't feel peace either way.

I decided I wouldn't go and told my husband I just didn't want to drive that far alone. A day or two later, I woke up and heard His voice. He called me to that mountain. I could hear Him say, "I need you on the mountain. It's not for you but for someone there." I thought to myself, *Am I crazy?* But it would not leave me. Every day, I heard the mandate. The call. *Go, go, go to that mountain.* When the time came, I packed my bags and drove the nine hours solo. I had no idea what to expect, nor did I know what I was supposed to do. All I knew was to be quiet and listen.

I attended the retreat, the services were wonderful, my spirit was fed, and it was coming to an end. I couldn't understand why the Lord called me to the mountain because it was almost over and nothing really happened that I would say was a mandate marker.

But then!

The last hour of the conference was baptisms. There were ladies lined up down the side of the mountain to be baptized in the hot tub in the Smoky Mountains. I watched and prayed, then I felt a tap on my shoulder. A lady named Beth asked me, "Would you mind to go back inside and pray with my granddaughter, Heather?" I replied, "Sure," and off I went. There were literally only five to six people left in the building.

I walked over to the young lady that was sitting alone and she began to cry. The Momma Jesus gifting came out and I held her while she wept. I asked her why she wanted me to pray for her. She told me out of everyone there she felt a pull to me and she wanted to rededicate her life to the Lord. I knew in that moment why I was sent to the mountain. It was for a young lady named Heather that saw the light in me and decided she too wanted to have the same light.

We prayed together and she rededicated her life to Christ. The conference was over and she said, "I know everything is over, but will you baptize me?" I was still in my church clothes so I went and got my T-shirt and shorts out of my car. Just us two went to the hot tub, then others joined around for prayer. She rededicated her life and then we baptized her in water.

What a renewal and refreshing came upon her. We all prayed and cried together. You see, I thought I had missed the voice of God. But, I didn't. I was waiting on Heather to move and it happened in His perfect timing.

I say this in all humbleness, for humility is who Jesus is...

To know out of 250 women He chose me for Heather is truly miraculous. He gave me a mandate to drive nine hours, attend a two-day conference, and when it was almost over, my mandate to the mountain was commissioned. A soul saved, baptized, and changed forever because I was willing to say Yes to Jesus. No matter what it costs me, I will Go. If I wasn't obedient, would Heather be back in a relationship with Jesus? Who knows, but I know this: He called me to the mountain for Heather. I would do it all over again for a soul. Souls matter, and if no one else seems to care, I DO!

# Chapter 10
## KINGDOM ASSIGNMENTS

Attached to each of our names is a Kingdom Assignment. It may take us days, months, or even years to discover what that assignment may be, but if we seek to know, He will show us.

God didn't create us to sit around and do nothing. He created us to serve, work, worship, and win souls. Each task we are called to do we should do it unto the Lord. "And whatever you do, do it heartily, as to the Lord and not to men, knowing that from the Lord you will receive the reward of the inheritance; for you serve the Lord Christ" (Colossians 3:23-24, NKJV).

As we walk in our journey with Christ, we go through different assignments. We may stay in one assignment longer than others, but we are to stay dedicated to that particular assignment until the Lord tells us it is complete.

I don't know about you, but I multitask. In my home I may start out doing dishes then halfway through end up in the laundry room. Next, I find myself making my bed and never finish the dishes. I call it multitasking but you could call it being distracted.

When we go from one thing to another, it's easy to get off course and never finish what we originally started. I do that with projects as well. I get so excited to paint a bedroom and redo it, then halfway through it, I'm over it and wonder why I even started out.

I'm sure I am not alone on this. Kingdom assignments can be the same. We are fired up and ready to go when we first feel the calling. The assignment seems right on target and we are excited. Then maybe after we fulfill this particular assignment for a while, we get burned out or even lose our joy.

Never once did Jesus tell us it would be easy, but He told us it would be worth it. I don't wake up every morning smiling and jumping around excited for the day. Most mornings I stumble to the kitchen, search for caffeine, then spend some time with the Lord. Until I get caffeine, I am basically sleepwalking. I get up all hours of the night with my special-needs daughter for she has assignments for me as well. The assignments never end!

### So what actually is a Kingdom Assignment?

Jeremiah 29:11 (NIV) says: " 'For I know the plans I have for you,' declares the Lord." His Kingdom assignments are two-fold: The first are the responsibilities He gives us as His children; and the second are specific assignments to every individual to fulfill our unique plans He has mapped out for our lives.

When He attaches an assignment to our life it comes with an inherent burden and a divinely given ability to solve problems that yield eternal value. It all boils down to adding value to the Kingdom. Whether it is soul winning, church planting, being a missionary, or whatever, it is an assignment the Lord grants to you as His child. He believes in you, therefore He attaches Kingdom assignments to your name.

On July 29 of 1997, I received the call of God on my life. I remember exactly where I was sitting and what I was doing. I heard Him attach an assignment to my life and I immediately felt unworthy, not equipped, and definitely not knowledgeable enough. But I heard Him and I knew. He quickly reminded me that if He calls me, He equips me.

He told me that I would minister to people all over the world. He called me a soul winner. I was so young at the time, I didn't grasp the call in fullness until years later. All I knew was I had a heart for Jesus and I loved people. That is a winning combination, for the Word tells us we must: walk in love. It's a commandment, not an option.

As time went on I had prophecies spoken over me and I saw them come to pass. One lady reminded me that my name was Kingdom assigned, for it is spelled C-H-R-I-S-T-I, Christ with an I. She told me every time she saw me that my name was personally assigned because I represented the Kingdom of God so well.

That meant so much to me and I have never forgotten it. I try my very best to be the ambassador of Christ He has called me to be. With my name representing Christ, my greatest desire is to reflect Him and lead others to the cross.

I think there are many people that have a calling on their life but have no idea what the assignment is for them. We find our assignments as we read the Word, spend time in prayer, ask questions, and prepare ourselves to allow quiet time for Him to speak to us.

I had a lady tell me one time that she couldn't hear the Lord speaking to her. She asked Him why and He gently replied, "Because you talk too much" That made me laugh, but if you think about it, that's so true. We go into our prayer closet, pray about everything we need to pray about, and then jump up, and we never gave the Spirit a chance to speak. I know I am guilty of that, but through maturing in my walk, I have learned to listen more than I talk. I think Jesus gave us two ears and one my mouth for a reason: listen more, talk less.

As I write this I stopped to read an email. The email had an attachment for me to open. I meditated on that and it is the same thing as the assignments attached to our life. Jesus gave us the assignment through His Word, correct? We are all called to minister, to share the Gospel of Jesus Christ. In Matthew 28:19-20 He tells us to "Go ye therefore and teach all the nations." We have an assignment right there to GO!

That is the responsibility of every believer. Then there are the specific assignments for eternal value, but what if you read the email but never opened the attachment? The attachment is where the assignment is.

I hear the Spirit speaking, "He is calling you to a specific assignment but you are yet to open the attachment." Maybe you are fearful like I was when I felt the call. Maybe you feel unqualified, but I am going to remind you again that He equips the called! He would not call you if He wasn't going to equip you. Think about that!

Would David have defeated Goliath if the Lord hadn't equipped him? Absolutely not! But David understood the assignment and was already prepared to defeat Goliath. David said to the Philistine in 1 Samuel 17:45, "You come against me with a sword and a spear and a shield but I come to you in the name of the Lord of hosts, the God of the armies of Israel, whom thou hast defiled" (CSB).

David knew that the Lord was with and for him. He declared aloud, "For the battle is the Lord's!" We have to remind ourselves daily that we are already equipped with His Spirit; we just have to know how to use the Word as our weapon. Every single thing the Lord is, has, or will call us to is for eternal value. He never allows us to go through a battle without a victory. If God is for us, and He is, who then can be against us? We must start walking in the boldness and authority of a Kingdom Heir for we are heirs with Christ.

***Romans 8:17 says, "Now if we are children, then we are heirs—heirs of God and co-heirs with Christ, if so be that we suffer with him, that we may be also glorified together" (NKJV).***

An heir is a partaker of the benefits that accompany salvation. Jesus did not die for Himself, but died for our benefits. As joint heirs we have access to the limitless resources of God Himself, the assurance of eternal life, and a relationship with Jesus that brings peace, love, and joy. Your divine assignment is to do what God wants you to do, have what God wants you to have, go where God wants you to go, and then become who God ultimately wants you to become.

Sometimes when you think of an assignment, it might take you to a time when you were in high school or college. The teacher or professor gave you an assignment to complete and typically it had a due date. I remember when my husband was in college. He was a huge procrastinator and waited until the last minute to get the assignment complete. He totally stressed himself and me out. I have no idea how he passed that particular class but he did.

There was never a reason to put off the assignment like that besides priorities being out of order and/or lazy. I think we can all be that way if we let things in life distract us. One thing I can tell you for sure is that laziness whether in school/college or in Kingdom assignments is not the will of God. When you are lazy in one area, it bleeds over into other areas. Laziness is a breeding ground for mediocrity and complacency.

God did not call us to a life of mediocrity but of exceeding abundance. We bring so much stress upon ourselves when we don't slow down and prioritize the important things in life. The Word tells us in Matthew 6:33, "But seek ye first the kingdom of God, and his righteousness, and all these things will be added to you" (KJV). That Scripture has a conjunction in it. You have to seek first AND THEN things will be added to you.

Maybe you don't do well in Kingdom assignments because you don't seek Him first. If you miss the very first instruction then none of the rest seems to matter. We always want to add on to our relationship with Christ, so let's not miss the added benefit by not seeking Him first. Jesus is the One who leads and guides us. When we try to follow our own path, we get lost along the way.

The enemy loves it when we become lazy and distracted, for that moves us away from our assignment. When we get our eyes on the world and off of the Kingdom, things take priority over our spiritual life. We must be so careful to not let our eyes get fixed on worldly things but keep our eyes fixed upon Jesus. "Fixing our eyes on Jesus, the pioneer and perfecter of faith" (Hebrews 12:2, NIV).

**Glance at your problems and keep your gaze upon Jesus.**

God's promises never expire, but I do believe there is a "due date" for Kingdom assignments. I say that because the Lord operates in divine order. He is not a God of chaos. When He calls us to a particular assignment, the Spirit guides us with complete instruction.

Just as a woman carries a baby in her womb for nine months, she is given a due date for delivery. If she never delivered the baby, new life would never be born. I have two children so I know exactly what it is like to carry them. It is a lot of work, change, and sacrifice to prepare your body for delivery. Just as in Kingdom assignments, it takes a lot of study, prayer, fasting, and listening to be able to complete and deliver what He has asked us to do.

Always remember: God is a promise keeper. When He calls us to an assignment, He gives us the grace to complete it in His appointed time and His timing is perfect!

# Afterword

Life is full of radiant colors to behold. Just as an artist uses a palette to create arrays of shades, so is our life. Our Creator has made each of us unique. Whether it's a twist, a turn or a myriad of colors, we are all a Kaleidoscope. Others may see fragments of our life, but Jesus sees the original Masterpiece that He created.

"For we are God's masterpiece. He has created us anew in Christ Jesus, so we can do the good things he planned for us long ago." (Ephesians 2:10 NLT)

Declaration: I declare that I am blessed by God. I have God-given abilities to do exceedingly well in all that He has called me to do. The Lord opens to me His good treasure, the heavens to give the rain to my land in its season and to bless the work of my hand. I am confident of this very thing, that He who begun a good work in me will complete it until the day of Jesus Christ.

# About the Author

Christi Johnston is an ordained minister with the Associated Brotherhood of Christians. She has been an evangelist, teacher of the Word, revivalist, conference speaker, and associate pastor. She is a certified mentor through Trailblazers, and the founder of Daughters Arise Mentoring Network for women.

She is the author or two previous books, Love Language: *A Mother's Heart and a Daughter's Unspoken Love,* and *I Know Who I Am: Walking in Your True Identity with Christ in Order to Live Your Best Life*. Christi is a natural-born leader and encourager, as she inspires others to walk in the fullness of their callings. Her life's mission is to lead others to the cross as they encounter the saving power of Jesus Christ.

Made in the USA
Columbia, SC
08 October 2024